The Beanie

Family Album
and Collector's Guide

By Shawn Brecka

ANTIQUE TRADER BOOKS
A DIVISION OF
LANDMARK SPECIALTY PUBLICATIONS
NORFOLK, VIRGINIA

DEDICATION

This book is dedicated to my daughter, Kendra Lane.

ISBN: 0-930625-95-1
Library of Congress Catalog Card Number: 98-72154

Editor: Allan W. Miller
Designer: Heather Ealey
Copy Editor: Sandra Holcombe

Printed in the United States of America

Beanie Babies is a registered trademark of Ty Inc. Full O' Beans is a trademark of Avon Products, Inc. Beanpals name, logos, and designs are copyrighted works of Kellytoy® and are registered trademarks of Kellytoy® U.S.A. Inc. Bean Sprouts is a registered trademark of Great American Fun and Gift Innovations. Chef Jr. Bean Bag Buddies is a registered trademark of International Home Foods, Inc. Clifford and the Clifford logo are registered trademarks of Scholastic Inc. Coca-Cola, Coke, the design of the contour bottle, and the design of the Coca-Cola Polar Bear are registered trademarks of The Coca-Cola Company. Disney trademarks and logos are proprietary to Disney Enterprises, Inc. "Energizer" is a registered trademark of Eveready Battery Company, Inc. The Breakfast of Champions, Cheerios, Honey Nut Cheerios, Cocoa Puffs, Trix, and Lucky Charms are registered trademarks of General Mills, Inc. Gund and all trademarks are the exclusive property of Gund Inc. Hallmark and Hallmark crown are trademarks of Hallmark Cards, Inc. Harley-Davidson is a registered trademark of Harley-Davidson. Kellogg's and related cereal names and character names are registered trademarks of Kellogg Company. McDonald's and the McDonaldland characters and names are registered trademarks of the McDonald's corporation and its affiliates. Meanies, all Meanies characters, names, related designs, slogans and limericks are registered trademarks of TOPKAT, L.L.C. NBC and the NBC Peacock are registered trademarks of the National Broadcasting Company. Rugrats, Rugrats logo and characters are properties of Nickelodeon. Precious Moments, Precious Moments Pals, and Precious Moments Tender Tails are registered trademarks of Precious Moments, Inc. Puffkins is a registered trademark of Swibco Inc. Sesame Street and the Sesame Street signs are trademarks of Children's Television Network. Sesame Street characters are copyrighted Jim Henson Productions, Inc. Warner Brothers, Warner Brothers logos and characters are trademarks and copyright by Warner Brothers.

All other trademarks presented in this book are the property of the respective trademark owners.

Information and opinions in this book represent the work of the author, and are in no way associated with, authorized, or endorsed by the respective trademark owners.

To order additional copies of this book,
or to obtain a catalog, please contact:

Antique Trader Books
P.O. Box 1050
Dubuque, Iowa 52004
or call 1-800-334-7165

The Beanie

Family Album

and Collector's Guide

CONTENTS

ACKNOWLEDGEMENTS

A huge thank you to my wonderful husband, Jon, for supporting me and encouraging me.

I would like to thank the following people for their input, support, and feedback:
Lynn Brecka, Shirl Furger, Allan Miller, Heather Ealey, Sandra Holcombe, Elizabeth Smith, Tracy Anderson, Amy Rohr, Rhonda Witwer, Ruth Tervelt, and Joan Welsh.

Special thanks to:
Susan Peters for allowing me to photograph her wonderful collection of Beanie Babies.
Cate & Company, Hwy QQ in King, Wisconsin, for selling wonderful bean-filled plush and always being generous and helpful.
Dylan Wilson, at Liquid Blue, makers of the Grateful Dead Beanie Bears.
James Pruden, at Avon, makers of the Avon Full O'Beans.
Richard Carlson, Hooked on Toys, at Toycarlson@aol.com.

THE BEANIE FAMILY ALBUM

When I began this book, I was thinking in terms of creating a Beanie Baby price guide. After all, Beanie Babies were the phenomenon of 1997, and they continue to be so today. But as I looked at the marketplace and saw how many people were interested in all sorts of different beanies, there was no way I could limit it to just Beanie Babies. Now you know why this book is entitled *The Beanie Family Album.*

I must admit to getting a late start in beanie collecting, having bought my first Beanie Baby in early 1997. But I was bitten hard by the beanie bug and have been aggressively collecting all sorts of beanies since then. And there are many, many different kinds of beanies out there. More are produced every week, and it's an almost impossible challenge to keep on top of all the happenings in the beanie hobby. Staying current on all the new releases is what I've done. You could say that this book is the "beans" of my labor.

The Beanie Family Album is the most comprehensive beanie guide available to collectors and dealers. It contains pictures, listings and prices of the most popular beanies today, including Beanie Babies, Disney, Beanpals, Puffkins, Bean Sprouts, advertising beanies, and many others. The goal of this book is twofold:

1. To identify, list, and place values on beanie toys.

2. To showcase beanies that many of you might not have been aware of—beanies that you might want to add to your collection.

I firmly believe that you will find this book to be an invaluable resource to help you better enjoy buying, selling, and collecting beanies. Getting enjoyment out of your beanies should be the top priority in your collecting pursuits.

And, no, there's nothing wrong with being happy that a beanie you bought for $5 is now worth $15, $50, or more than $100. That's great! You should take pride in owning something that not all collectors own, but wish they did. And, no, there's nothing wrong with selling your beanies for a profit. You should feel good that you made such a wise purchase in the first place.

But always keep in mind that you should *enjoy* your beanies. Display them and play with them (be careful if you play with your valuable ones). Don't get upset if you don't get a newly released beanie right away. Chances are pretty strong that you will get the beanie you want at a reasonable price in a few weeks or a month. So enjoy the beanies you have, and enjoy hunting for the ones you don't have. It isn't life or death. It's supposed to be fun. When you look at the beanies displayed in your house or child's room, they should make you smile. I know my beanies make me happy.

Good luck in finding the beanies you're looking for, and be kind to other collectors (especially young collectors).

Shawn Brecka
December 1997

Collecting Beanies

INTRODUCTION

The story of the year for 1997 in the collectibles arena was a hands-down, slam-dunk for Beanie Babies (as well as for all bean-filled toys). Without a doubt the most popular thing since sliced bread, hundreds of thousands of people (probably more than a million and maybe even more than two or three million) descended on small gift shops all across the country to buy Beanie Babies. The number of new Beanie Baby collectors was something to behold. A new and ever-growing marketplace literally blossomed overnight, with millions and millions of dollars changing hands, along with small bean-filled toys.

Children and adults were equally captivated by Beanie Babies. Children brought their prized Beanie Babies to school; in some instances, Beanie Babies were banned from schools because they caused such a ruckus in the classroom. Adults collected them with fervor, checking off their checklists and making daily trips to their favorite Beanie Baby hangouts. The Internet buzzed with Beanie Baby sales. Conventions were held and clubs were formed. Was America ready for Beanie Babies? Yes, it was! And all signs point toward continued strength in the Beanie Baby market for years to come.

AREN'T BEANIE BABIES JUST A FAD?

One of the most often-asked questions I get about Beanie Babies is: "Aren't they just a fad toy like Tickle Me Elmo or Cabbage Patch dolls?" For those who are not involved in this hobby, it's a reasonable question that deserves a reasonable response.

I don't believe that collecting beanies is a fad. Here's why:

1. Beanie Babies have demonstrated strength for an extended period of time in the market, on both the retail and secondary market levels; that's one clue that they aren't a fad. Beanie Babies have a sales history of more than four years; in addition, secondary market values have remained strong. The gains realized in Beanie Babies in 1997 haven't been lost. In a fad-type environment, prices rise and fall very quickly. Values for the most desirable styles did rise quickly in 1997 (refer to the graphs in the Beanie Babies section), but there have been no noteworthy declines to date.

2. Beanie Babies and other types of bean-filled plush are collected by both adults and children. They are a toy *and* a collectible (they are, however, more of a collectible than a toy at this time). In many ways, they are similar to Hot Wheels cars and Barbie dolls. Hot Wheels and Barbies are collected by adults and played with by children. In the case of most fad toys, they are geared toward children, and only children have an interest in them. For example, Power Rangers had a great appeal to youngsters who watched the television show, but the show was too silly for most adults. Children wanted the toys and adults obliged them. When children were no longer interested in the show or the toys, there was no one left to pick up the slack. The fad passed, and interest in Power Rangers today is minimal. Beanies, on the other hand, had a great appeal to adult collectors from the beginning. Look at how many different lines of teddy bears and the like are collected by adults. If you think of beanies in the same way you think about Precious Moments or Hallmark Ornaments, you can begin to understand what they've actually become.

3. Most current beanies are inexpensive and available. Sure, there are some Beanie Babies and Walt Disney Mini Bean Bags that are hard to get or expensive, but the majority of them are priced at $5 to $6 each, and most stores have them in stock. Fad toys tend to be those that are hard to get. The fewer there are, the more that people want them. When a fad toy is finally produced in large quantities, few people want them (there were more than enough Tickle Me Elmos to go around for the holiday season in 1997). Most beanies have been produced in ample quantities now and are readily available. Still, however, they are selling at a steady pace. That's good news for the future.

4. Beanies are peaceful, cute, cuddly, non-threatening, and they make people happy. That's the best reason to collect anything—because it makes you happy. The timing must

have been right for Beanie Babies to rise in popularity the way they did. Many toys in the 1990s marketplace are aggressive and violent. Perhaps collectors gravitated toward bean-filled plush partly in response to moving away from the violence-related toys. This is a whole philosophical question that probably has some merit. Did anyone discuss this when pogs or Power Rangers were the hot toys? Nope! In other words, don't expect to see a sudden change from cute and cuddly Beanie Babies to gun-toting, war-loving Beanie Babies in the future.

For these reasons, I certainly don't believe beanies are a fad toy. To me, they're both a legitimate collectible and a toy. My baby daughter has three or four Beanie Babies that she plays with (Snip is her favorite). I even let her rip the tags off a Velvet (after Velvet had been retired!).

I foresee beanie plush following in the footsteps of Barbie dolls. I think the appeal of Beanie Babies and many other lines of bean-filled characters is strong enough that adults will continue to collect them and children who are playing with and collecting them now will continue to buy them in the future. To accomplish this, beanies have to maintain their toy appeal and not become strictly a collectible. That means that the retail price must remain around $5 or $6 so that children can purchase them with their allowance money. They must also maintain this price so that people can give them as nice, inexpensive gifts for birthdays and holidays.

They must remain readily available (not overproduced, but produced in quantities that approach the demand level). Finally, parents need to let their children play with some of the beanies. Don't fret if a hang tag gets creased or chewed off. If children are going to grow up to collect Beanie Babies, they must be allowed to have memories of playing with them. Would adults collect Barbies or trains today if they didn't get to play with the ones they had when they were younger? Probably not.

Whether you're an adult collector or a child who likes playing with the array of different beanies out there, the main thing to remember is to have fun with them. Don't take them too seriously. Take them for what they are—fun, little, soft, colorful stuffed toys filled with little plastic beans.

A LOOK AT 1998 AND BEYOND

What does the future hold for beanies? Rumors are swirling about massive new releases and massive impending retirements for Beanie Babies. What's going to happen is anyone's guess. What I can tell you at this point is that the new-release rumors are seldom true, while the retirement rumors are almost never true. If you spend any amount of time on the Internet, you'll find posts from collectors who swear they got information direct from a good source that some particular event is going to happen. Rarely do these rumors come to pass. Don't base your buying decisions on rumors. Use common sense.

Some are predicting that there may be massive changes in the colors of Beanie Babies (not retirements, but distinct color changes), which could fuel the hobby for the next several years. Mystic was given an iridescent horn in November of 1997; this variation caused a good stir in the market. I hope this Mystic change is the first of many that Ty creates. A lot of collectors already have all the current styles: there's nothing left for them to collect, except for new releases and high-priced retirees. Changing the colors would usher in a new era for collectors. Wouldn't it be fun if Peanut was issued in a couple of different colors next year? I'd buy them. I don't, however, have a good reason to buy another light blue Peanut for my collection.

Others are speculating that Ty will introduce several specially made limited-edition Beanie Babies that will sell for much more than the current retail average price of $5. And watch for Disney to release many more Mini Bean Bags. Nineteen ninety-eight could be a heck of a year!

In 1998, look for more fake and altered Beanie Babies to come out of the woodwork. In 1997, there were several possible scams, including someone surgically removing Quacker's wings to turn him into a wingless Quacker; someone removing Spot's spot; and a whole slew of fake Grunts. The people making these fake and altered Beanie

Babies will get better at making them, so be on your guard in 1998. As Beanie Baby prices have soared, so have the instances of deception. Watch out for deals that are too good to be true, and buy your Beanie Babies from quality dealers and individuals only. If you happen to get a fake from a quality seller, he or she will refund your money. If you get your fake from a fly-by-nighter, forget about it.

Collectors are hoping that distribution of new Beanie Babies improves in 1998, since 1997 was totally frustrating for those who were trying to get their hands on new releases. It was a shame that distribution wasn't better, because Ty made some of its finest Beanie Babies in 1997. Many retailers were also frustrated, as they had to keep telling their customers, "No, we haven't gotten the new releases in yet." As of December, collectors and retailers in many parts of the country still hadn't gotten a Peace, which was a May 1997 release.

Because distribution has been so poor (and the fact that collectors have proven time and time again that they will pay well above the retail price for new styles), many retailers have begun sales practices that are giving collectors a headache:

1. Dealers are charging more for new, hard-to-get releases. I know of one long-time collector who decided to quit collecting Beanie Babies and to sell the ones she had because the store she buys them from wouldn't sell her any at the normal $5. This store, of which she thought she was a valued customer, was charging more than $10 for the new releases. This was the straw that broke the camel's back in the case of that collector.

2. The second way retailers are causing problems with secondary market prices is by taking all the new releases they get and selling them to secondary market dealers and/or auctioning or selling them on the Internet.

Either way, these practices spell trouble for hobbyists looking for new beanies. Logic tells us that if collectors didn't pay exorbitant prices for new releases, these types of practices would cease; however, common sense says that most hobbyists collect with their hearts, not their minds. As long as Beanie Babies are a hot seller, there will be enough hobbyists collecting with their hearts to keep prices of new releases very high (at least in the first weeks or months of release). This is just human nature.

This whole situation will be solved if beanies are produced in decent quantities and distributed quickly. If this doesn't happen, then hopefully more collectors will begin to collect with their minds and exercise patience when it comes to new releases. Just think about how many times you thought you'd never see a particular style, only to see it out in good numbers a month later. It happens all the time. Collectors who spend a great deal of money on what turns out to be a common Beanie Baby are likely candidates to leave the hobby.

Another situation that cropped up (mostly after the September 1997 retirements) was retailers selling newly retired Beanie Babies for $10 to $25; these were mostly Beanie Babies that were sent to them after the retirement announcements were made. While charging a premium for newly retired styles is another instance that upsets some collectors, it doesn't seem to me to be as negative as selling new releases for those same prices. Ten dollars for a retired Beanie Baby, even a common one, is a fair price.

Some retailers limit the number of hard-to-get or newly retirees to one or two, and charge their normal $5 or $6; this keeps one individual from buying all the desirable Beanie Babies and it lets more collectors get them. Bravo to the retailers with these policies! Other retailers have started Beanie Baby punchcards that allow collectors to "earn" a retired or hard-to-get style after purchasing a specific number of Beanie Babies. The retailers I've talked to about this told me this has worked well and that collectors appreciate getting a hard-to-find style. It's a win-win situation, in which the retailer sells more Beanie Babies and collectors get something they want.

Many people are using Beanie Babies in auctions or raffles to raise money for charitable causes. Some collectors donate their extra Beanie Babies to children's hospitals to brighten up the day of children with serious health problems. There are other opportunities for win-win situations in the hobby in 1998. Let's take advantage of each one we can.

ARE BEANIES A GOOD INVESTMENT?

This book doesn't give a lot of investment advice on beanies. No one can predict with any degree of accuracy what a Beanie Baby or other beanie-style character is going to be worth a year, five years or 10 years from now. If someone says they know, realize that it's simply not possible to know future values of beanies (or anything else, for that matter). Some people have tried. While these forecasts might be fun to look at, they should not be taken seriously.

But things aren't that simple. So many factors will affect the future:

- Will new styles be introduced, and then be retired quickly?

- Will the collector be catered to, by seeing more style and color changes?

- Will Ty continue to produce the same styles in large quantities? If Beanie Babies get severely overproduced, who will have an interest in buying them for more than $5?

- Will today's bean-filled plush collectors stay in the hobby or will many leave? People's tastes can change over time. Figural alcohol decanters, fruit jars, and telephone insulators were big in the 1970s. Where are they now? Nowhere.

- Will more people begin collecting beanies over the next few years? Will the introduction of the Ty Princess bear draw a lot of new Beanie Baby collectors? Will another promotion, like McDonald's Teenie Beanie Baby promotion, be the hit of the summer?

- Will children maintain their interest in Beanie Babies?

- What will the economy be like? Does anyone think that beanies wouldn't be affected by a recession?

As I said, the question of investing in bean-filled plush is not a simple one.

With that said, my best investment advice is not to invest in beanies. That's right! Don't *invest* in them. Invest your money in things that have proven to be good investments over a long period of time, such as mutual funds. Don't take money you plan to use for your child's education and sink it into beanies. The money you spend on beanies should be your discretionary funds—money you do can without, whether it's $10 a month to buy two little creatures, or $500 a month to buy retirees.

I'm not predicting that the beanies won't rise in value in the coming years. I think there is a good possibility they might very well continue to prosper in value. But don't expect the kinds of gains that the hobby saw in 1997 ever again. With exceptions, don't think that you can buy a bunch of currents for $5 each and sell them for $10 or $15 the next day. At this time, with the supply at strong levels, those good old days are over.

To illustrate how spectacular 1997 was, consider that some Beanie Babies went from less than $100 to almost $1,000 in just 12 months—that's a 1,000% increase! Others experienced the same kinds of percentage increases. If you bought Beanie Babies at the beginning of 1997, or before, you were very smart. But you certainly didn't buy them thinking that they'd rise tenfold in value in a year (okay, maybe there was one or two of you out there). Most Beanie Babies you're buying today will not increase at astronomical rates. Sure, some Beanie Babies will leap in value for one reason or another in 1998, but not the entire Beanie Baby line.

When collectibles are viewed in mere dollar amounts, it won't be long until those collectibles become worthless. Buy beanies because you like them, not because you think they'll make you money. That's the advice you'll get from any good antiques or collectibles dealer. These dealers also say that if you buy what you like, you'll almost always wind up making money. It's funny how it works, but the making-money part of this equation seems to take care of itself when you buy what you like. On the other hand, you'll likely seal your fate of losing money if you buy what you think will be worth a lot of money in the future.

At this time, some collectors are cashing in their Beanie Babies, figuring now is the best opportunity to sell their collections, with Beanie Babies as hot as they've ever been. They're following the simple buy low/sell high principle of economics. Expect to see more older retirees for sale over the next 12 months, especially the January and May 1997 retirees. While there might be more retirees for sale, there will probably be plenty of eager collectors buying them, ensuring that values will remain strong. Just a few of the September 1997 retirees (notably Tank, Seamore, and the brown Teddy), and a couple of December retirees (Snowball and 1997 Teddy) are on want lists. Collectors who joined the beanie fray after the May 1997 retirement announcements have most of the currents and latest retirees. It would take another large influx of new collectors for the more common September and December 1997 retirees to jump up significantly in value.

For all the reasons I've stated, I've chosen instead to offer a smattering of buying advice, along with graphs that track retired Beanie Baby values for 1997. I've outlined what I call "if" situations—for instance, "if" Ty retires Blizzard soon, he will become a valuable style. In future editions of this guide, when other bean-filled plush lines have market-value track records, I'll include graphs and more buying advice for them, too. Use this information and your own common sense when buying beanies.

ENJOYING YOUR COLLECTION

You must enjoy your beanie collection! And that's an order! It isn't a tall order, though. Enjoying your beanies is the easy part of collecting them.

How you take pleasure from your collection is up to you. Many folks are working on getting a complete set of all current Beanie Babies. When this task is complete, they often go back to buy as many retirees as they can afford. Some collect just the farm-related animals. Others concentrate on the cats, dogs, African animals or teddy bears. It's up to you as to how you want to customize your collection.

Display your beanies. I put ours on shelves—it's sweet and simple. Some collectors place them in display cases, while others put them in baskets. My sister-in-law has assembled a collection that she displays in a Noah's Ark theme.

Some Beanie Babies are so valuable, however, that you probably should not be handling them a lot. For these expensive Beanie Babies, look into purchasing specially made cases that protect them from the elements. Hang-tag protectors might also be a good idea, since the Beanie Baby tags are a big key to the value. I would advise against storing beanies in air-tight plastic bags that could promote humidity and cause damage. If your collection is especially valuable, contact your insurance agent, and be sure they are properly insured. That's right! Insure your beanie collection!

What's the best way to buy current beanies? In lean times, it's tough to find beanies anywhere. In good times, they're everywhere. I have found that if you consistently buy your beanies from just a few sources, it's beneficial. If you can develop an ongoing relationship with your local or mail-order retailer, that retailer is more likely to hold tough-to-find styles for you. Loyalty is often rewarded. Trading is also a good way to build your collection. Find collectors in your area who are interested in trading with you.

Buying retirees is another matter. Beanie Baby conventions are popping up all the time. Obviously, this is one of the best places to find retirees. You can find dealers in collectibles magazines and on the Internet. The Internet also has places you can find Beanie Baby auctions (two of the larger are at "eBay" and "up4sale"). When buying through the mail, be extra cautious. There are a few individuals who are not on the up-and-up. Get references, and check them.

RETIREMENTS VS. STYLE CHANGES

Retiring collectible items is not new. Makers of other limited edition items have been retiring their items for a number of years. Retiring an item gives it more collectibility, since the item will no longer be produced. Ty made the retirements of Beanie Babies a big production on its Internet site. Collectors had a lot of fun trying to guess which styles would be the next to go. Retirement meant higher prices for Beanie Babies. For example, when Garcia retired, his value went from $5 to $15 to more than $50 overnight. Be advised, however, that retirement doesn't mean a particular style won't keep appearing on retailer shelves for weeks or even months after the announcement. Flip, Speedy, and Velvet (retired Sept. 30, 1997) were found in shipments as late as December 1997.

From Jan. 1, 1997, and on, Ty's retirements have been announced via the Internet. Again, a retirement is an official ending of production of a particular style and name. Style changes are not considered retirements. Here are examples that illustrate the differences:

Retirement: The Beanie Baby, Kiwi, was retired in January 1997. That means that Ty will not produce a Beanie Baby with the name "Kiwi" again in the same color as Kiwi. In the future, Ty might issue a Beanie Baby in the same style as Kiwi, but the new Beanie Baby will have a different name and new colors.

Style change: Mystic the unicorn (Beanie Baby) was originally issued with a tan horn. Ty decided to change Mystic's horn to an iridescent color. That was a style change. Even though Ty has not produced Mystic with a tan horn for some time (and likely never will again), the tan-horn Mystic has not been officially retired, even though she is, for all intents and purposes, retired. The tan-horn Mystic is referred to as "discontinued." The iridescent-horn Mystic is known as "current," as in "current style" or currently available."

VALUES FOR DIFFERENT CONDITIONS

You bought a Beanie Baby for your child—it was Slither the snake, in fact—and your little munchkin played with Slither and tore the hang tag off. So what's it worth now? A lot of people are surprised that retired Beanie Babies that are not in near mint or mint condition are still valuable. The main reason that non-mint older retirees have value is that there are so few perfect ones available that collectors are willing to buy imperfect examples (this is another sign that the beanie market is very strong).

Here are some general condition factors and how they affect prices:

MINT: A perfect beanie. It has all of its tags without creases. There are no factory defects. The prices in this guide are "mint" prices.

NEAR MINT: An almost perfect beanie. Often, what makes a mint version into a near mint version is a slightly bent, but not creased, hang tag. Valued at 80% to 90% of the mint price.

EXCELLENT: This beanie appears to be mint, but it has a crease in its hang tag. Valued at 65% to 75% of the mint price.

VERY GOOD: A beanie that's missing its hang tag, but is otherwise in superb condition. May have been lightly played with. Valued at 45% to 60% of the mint price.

LESS THAN VERY GOOD: Beanies that have been heavily played with are valued at anywhere from 5% to 35% of the mint price, depending on the damage. Damage can include worn fabric, tears, repairs, stains, missing eyes, and other bad things that detract from overall appearance.

Note: If you own a current and easy-to-find beanie that is in less than near-mint condition, it's likely that you will be unable to sell it at the above-listed percentages. The reason is that if a collector can easily find a mint beanie for $5, he or she is highly unlikely to pay you $2 or $3 for one that's missing its hang tag.

ABOUT THE VALUES IN THIS GUIDE

The values for the different types of beanies in this guide have been arrived at through various collectors' and dealers' sales lists and auction results from all across the United States. They are average secondary market prices for mint beanies. This price is what you can expect to pay for a beanie from a seller, whether that seller is a dealer or a collector. If you were selling your beanies to a dealer, the price he or she would pay could range from 40% to 80% of the secondary market value, depending on the beanie and the dealer. Oftentimes, you can get more for your beanies from individual collectors, as they don't have to factor-in profit when buying.

The values in this book should be used as a guide. In 1998, prices for some beanies will increase far above the values listed in this book, due to retirements, style changes, and other unpredictable factors. Prices for some beanies might decrease. Keep these things in mind when using this guide.

Manufacturing mistakes: Occasionally, beanies are produced with errors, such as one too many or too few legs, a missing tail, and so on. These errors, if legitimate, are of interest to collectors (some collectors might even specialize in error beanies). There is no good way to put a value on these mutant beanies. The best way to sell error versions would be at an auction.

Tag errors: Many times, hang tags and tush tags don't end up on the correct beanies. For instance, a Beanie Baby Legs' tush tag might have been sewn on Gracie at the point of manufacture. Generally, these errors are not of great interest to collectors. In fact, with the proper equipment, hang tags can easily be switched. Tush tags, on the other hand, are of a little more interest to collectors, as these are not so easily switched. My advice is not to pay any premium for a hang-tag error (easily faked). Tush-tag errors, except in a few instances (notably the Beanie Baby Maple with a Pride tush tag), are generally valued at $5 more than the price of a correctly tagged version.

The Beanie Family Album

A&W Beanie Bear

The famous A&W Bear was issued in beanie form in late 1997. He's cool as a frosty mug of A&W Root Beer, with his orange hat and sweater and hard-plastic A&W logo attached to his chest. He stands 6 1/2 inches high and is sold in a plastic bag.

Tags: Only a tush tag that reads "Alpha Kids."

Availability: Without an A&W in my local area, I had to buy mine from another collector. I did hear that these were sold as premiums at A&W restaurants for $1.99.

Average retail price: $10

Future collectibility: There are a great many dedicated A&W collectors who will be going after this cute bear, so the future looks good. It isn't known at this time if the bear was produced in large numbers, but I would suspect not, since the secondary market prices seem strong. Like many of these one-beanie sets, future collectibility may depend on whether or not A&W will continue to issue other types and styles of A&W Bear beanies in the future. If A&W does continue its bean-oriented collectibles line, that will almost certainly make this first beanie more desirable.

A&W Beanie Bear

A&W Bear—with orange hat and sweater; current value: $10

AVON FULL O' BEANS

Avon, which has begun marketing more toys of late, jumped into the beanie toy market with the introduction of a half-dozen Full O' Beans in November of 1997. Very well executed, Full O' Beans are a high-quality product that every beanie collector should consider. Each measures about 9 inches long. It isn't known at this time what Avon plans to do as far as retiring certain styles. If retirements occur, expect the retired styles to become more valuable, perhaps around $8 to $12.

Tags: The hang tags are kidney-bean shaped, and contain each Full O' Bean's name, birthday, and a poem.

Availability: Through your Avon representative.

Average retail price: $4.99

Related Internet site: Avon-http://www.avon.com

Future collectibility: Because of the quality of this line, Full O' Beans gets a big endorsement from this author. At this time, this is a nice small set of beanies that happens to be affordable. Of all the Full O' Beans, the orange bear would seem to have the most appeal, as there are many collectors who specialize in bears.

"Bernard"

"Zoe"

"Lenny"

"Jumbo"

"Dapper"

Avon Full O' Beans Characters

Bernard the Bear—released: December 1997; birthday: December 21; current value: $5

Dapper the Dinosaur—released: February 1998; birthday: May 14; current value: $5

Juggler the Seal—released: December 1997; birthday: January 20; current value: $5

Jumbo the Elephant—released: December 1997; birthday: May 10; current value: $5

Lenny the Leopard—released: December 1997; birthday: September 17; current value: $5

Mozzarella the Mouse—released: January 1998; birthday: July 17; current value: $5

Rumply the Sharpei—released: December 1997; birthday: March 15; current value: $5

Skips the Puppy—released: December 1997; birthday: August 4; current value: $5

Stretch the Giraffe—released: January 1998; birthday: June 9; current value: $5

Zoe the Zebra—released: February 1998; birthday: February 14; current value: $5

"Rumply"

"Juggler"

"Mozzarella"

"Skips"

"Stretch"

BEANIE BABIES & TEENIE BEANIE BABIES

WHERE BEANIE BABIES BEGAN

Bean-filled toys are nothing new. In fact, they've "bean" around for 20 years or more. But there's a Grand Canyon's worth of difference between bean-filled toys and Beanie Babies.

Beanie Babies are the invention of Ty Warner, of Ty Inc., which is headquartered in Oakbrook, Illinois. Beanie Babies were first available for sale to the public in 1994, and they were sold mostly in the Chicago area. Nine different styles were originally made: Chocolate the moose, Cubbie the bear, Flash the dolphin, Legs the frog, Patti the platypus, Pinchers the lobster, Splash the whale, Spot the dog and Squealer the pig. The Ty beanies were sold through small specialty floral and gift shops, including Hallmark stores; they were not sold through major retail stores. Even today (with a few exceptions), these small gift shops are the only places you can find Beanie Babies.

The current Beanie Baby craze began in earnest in early 1997, when Ty "officially" retired several styles of Beanie Babies at its new mega-popular Internet site at "ty.com" (by the way, this site went over the billion-hit mark in late 1997). Before that time, the company merely stopped offering the styles for sale. Within the first few months of 1997, the Beanie Baby train was rolling and there was nothing to stop it. Retirements in January, May, September, and December of 1997 caused values to rise and more people to become interested in collecting them. The initial secondary market prices for new Beanie Babies was sometimes more than $20, $50, or even $100, illustrating that people wanted their Beanie Babies, they wanted them now, and they were willing to pay for them!

The McDonald's Teenie Beanie Baby promotion in April of 1997 was a huge success (see the section "Beanie Babies: Teenie Beanie Babies"). This national promotion brought in thousands and thousands of new collectors, which only fanned the fire. During this time, there was scarcely a Beanie Baby to be had anywhere. Retailer shelves were wiped clean. New shipments were sold out in hours, as people waited in line outside stores to buy the elusive Beanie Babies. This supply situation improved throughout the year until it seemed that there were too many Beanie Babies around by the last half of 1997.

TAG IDENTIFICATION

Beanie Baby hang tags and tush tags have changed several times through the years. These tag differences help to determine when a Beanie Baby was manufactured.

Some collectors will pay more (sometimes, 10 to 20 times more) for early-style tags, even though the Beanie Baby itself is exactly the same as later-tagged versions. Other collectors aren't convinced that an old-tag Beanie Baby that's in the same style as a new-tag version is worth paying more for. Style 1 and 2 tags are not all that common. These were the tags that were on the Beanie Babies when they were still actually toys (1994-1995), so most of them got torn off. Yes, early tags are scarce. Are they worth more money? Yes. Are they worth collecting? As I mentioned, some say yes, and others say no. Buying a Beanie Baby for its tags is something that usually concerns advanced collectors. For example, an advanced collector might want to get a Chocolate with all five of the different style tags it was issued in. That would be a challenge. If you are going to sell a Chocolate (or other style) with an early tag, I suggest putting it up for bids.

Here are descriptions of the hang tags:

> **Style 1 hang tag (1994):** The first Beanie Babies had a single-sided hang tag. The front of the heart-shaped hang tag has the letters "ty" in lower case, in thin letters.

Style 2 hang tag (1994-1995): The second hang tag opened up like a book. The front was the same as Style 1.

Style 3 hang tag (1995-1996): The third hang tag has a re-designed heart shape, and much larger and fatter "ty" letters on the front. The inside remained the same.

Style 4 hang tag (1996-1997): A star with the words "Beanie Original Baby" was added to the front of the fourth hang tag. Birthdates and poems were added on the inside of the tags.

Style 5 hang tag (1997-present): Font used on tag was changed to a comic style.

Here's a history of the tush tags:

Style 1 tush tag (1993-1995): The first tush tag had black lettering.

Style 2 tush tag (1995-1996): The second tush tag had red lettering, along with the Ty heart logo.

Style 3 tush tag (1996-1997): The third tush tag looked the same as the second, but included the name of the Beanie Baby under the heart, and had "The Beanie Babies Collection" added above the heart.

Style 4 tush tag (1997): The fourth tush tag, introduced in mid-1997, was the same as the third, but a small star was added near the upper-left of the heart. Some of the small stars (early versions) were affixed on the tush tag with the star on clear tape, while the later versions had the star as part of the tag. A "TM" symbol was added on this tag by the name of the Beanie Baby in November 1997.

Canadian tush tags: Canadian Beanie Babies have two tush tags, with information printed in both English and French.

A word of warning: Many of the older, retired Beanie Babies were played with, and no longer have their hang tags. With the proper equipment, a hang tag from a new Beanie Baby could be placed on an old one that was missing its tag and be sold at the mint price. At the least, this behavior is unethical; at worst, it would seem it is outright fraud. The best advice is to pass on deals that don't seem right. If the seller makes you nervous, there's probably a reason for it. If the price is way too low, there's likely a reason it is too low. Know who you're dealing with. Know what you're buying.

WHERE TO FIND BEANIE BABY NEWS

There are many Internet sites that are great places to find the latest news on happenings in the Beanie Baby and beanbag toy world. The following Internet sites are some of the best sources for up-to-the-minute news, comments, and rumors:

BB World News and Information:
   http://www.geocities.com/EnchantedForest/3098/ index.html

Beanie Mom: http://www.beaniemom.com/

The Beanie Philes: http://www.beaniephiles.com/

RJW's Beanie Mania: http://www.beaniemania.com/index.html

Rosie Wells Enterprises, Inc.: http://www.rosiewells.com/

Ty Inc.: http://www.ty.com/

"1997 TEDDY" THE BEAR (R)

Born: 12 - 25 - 96
Released: Sept. 30, 1997
Retired: Dec. 31, 1997
Description: Rumored to be a forthcoming new release several weeks before he was officially announced as a new Beanie Baby in September 1997, the "1997 Teddy" has proven to be an instant classic, especially in light of his abrupt retirement. Initially, this brown bear with a stocking hat was tough to find. The first Teddys on the secondary market were selling from $75 to $150 in mid-October of 1997 (some collectors couldn't wait to be the first on their block to have one). The price went down to about $15 in December, but, upon retirement, he made a drastic upward jump. If Ty continues to ship large quantities of this retired BB over the first few months of 1998, his current value might come down a little. If not, look for higher prices throughout 1998 and beyond.
Value: $35.00

(No value chart is presented for this retired item due to its brief three-month production period.)

"ALLY" THE ALLIGATOR (R)

Born: 3 - 14 - 94
Released: 1994
Retired: Sept. 30, 1997
Description: It was no real surprise to collectors when Ally was announced as a retiree in September 1997—a style that had been around for years. Ally was available in abundance through 1997 and was a slow mover. But now that time has caught up with our old pal and he's collecting Social Security (or the BB equivalent), he is viewed a lot differently.
Value: $20.00

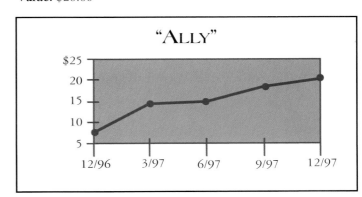

"BALDY" THE BALD EAGLE

Born: 2 - 17 - 96
Released: May 1997
Description: Will Baldy turn out to be a seasonal-type (July 4th) Beanie Baby who gets an early retirement, as did Libearty in 1997? Time will tell. If Ty bids adieu to Baldy in 1998, look for this beanie bird to soar high in value in the future. Whatever happens, Baldy will remain a popular character who'll fly off retailer shelves well into the future.
Value: $12.00

"BATTY" THE BAT

Born: 10 - 29 - 96
Released: Sept. 30, 1997
Description: Batty is significant in that he's the first Beanie Baby with Velcro. With Velcro on his wings, collectors can display their little bat in a variety of places. Announced just in time for the Halloween season (though not immediately widely available), it's uncertain how long Batty will remain a part of the Beanie Baby family, as he might be a seasonal offering.
Value: $15.00

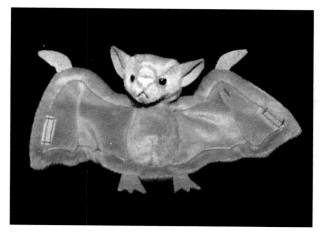

"BERNIE" THE ST. BERNARD

Born: 10 - 3 - 96
Released: January 1997
Description: A sad-looking dog, perhaps forlorn, Bernie was out in good quantities since his release, but toward the end of the year, it appeared his numbers had dwindled. Bernie is a middle-range popular Beanie Baby dog who'll become more popular once he retires.
Value: $10.00

"BESSIE" THE COW (R)

Born: 6 - 27 - 95
Released: 1995
Retired: Sept. 30, 1997
Description: Popular from the get-go, the brown and white Bessie was on the hard-to-get list for most of 1997, prompting speculation of an impending retirement. It happened in September 1997, and it turns out that Bessie is one of the more valuable retirees. Oddly enough, however, I saw Bessie in stores just twice in 1997 before her retirement. Since her retirement, I've seen her three times. I'd like to see the Bessie style come back soon. How about "Bossy" the red cow?
Value: $28.00

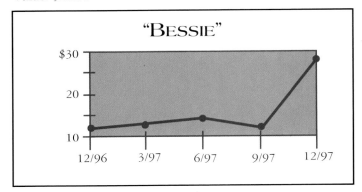

"BLACKIE" THE BEAR

Born: 7 - 15 - 94
Released: 1995
Description: The black version of Cubbie, Blackie is fast becoming an old Beanie Baby. Through much of 1997, Blackie was a tough one to find, prompting many to believe the end was approaching for him. However, he survived the December 1997 retirements and was out in good quantities in the last quarter of 1997.
Value: $10.00

"BLIZZARD" THE WHITE TIGER

Born: 12 - 12 - 96
Released: May 1997
Description: Blizzard provides a good case in point for when Beanie Baby rumors run amok. It wasn't long after this black and white tiger was released that the rumor-mill was churning out stories that Ty would have to change his name because Dairy Queen had an ice cream concoction that was called the "Blizzard." Yes, it was true that DQ had the "Blizzard," but it was not true, at least at this point in time, that Ty would have to change Blizzard's name, a la Doodle to Strut. Several new names were even mentioned for Blizzard, including Snowflake. Rumors aside, this tiger, as all the other Beanie Baby tigers/panthers/leopards, is a hugely popular style. If he should happen to meet an early retirement, he'll certainly become very valuable. He was not widely available in the last four months of 1997.
Value: $14.00

"BONES" THE DOG

Born: 1 - 18 - 94
Released: 1994
Description: Bones is one of the earliest Beanie Babies still around. He seems to be a favorite of children, perhaps because he has a more cartoon look about him than do the other Beanie Baby dogs. Bones was not spotted much for many months in 1997; but a bunch of Bones appeared in November. Is Bones ready for the Beanie pasture soon?
Value: $10.00

"BONGO"/"NANA" THE MONKEY

Born: 8 - 17 - 95
Released: 1995
Variations: tan tail (current), brown tail (current, but scarce), "Nana" variation (discontinued)
Description: An adored and classic Beanie Baby, Bongo was originally named Nana. The only difference between Nana and the current Bongo is the "Nana" hang tag and its black-and-white tush tag. Nana has a light tail. The Nana-tagged version is very rare, as you can see from its value. Bongo comes in two different versions: a tail that's the same color as its body, and a tail that's the same color as its face. It would appear that the dark-tail version (tail the same color as his body) is tougher to get; most of the Bongos out in the last half of 1997 have light tails. In fact, there is speculation that the dark-tailed version is discontinued, although I found a pair of dark-tailed Bongos in the first part of December that were mixed in with light-tailed versions.
Value: tan-tail "Bongo"—$12.00; brown-tail "Bongo"—$25.00; "Nana" version—$1,225.00

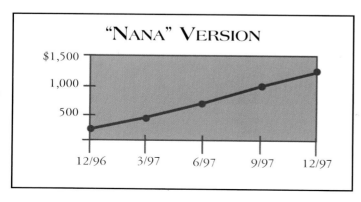

"BRONTY" THE BRONTOSAURUS (R)

Born: N/A
Released: 1995
Retired: 1996
Description: Bronty pulled the "now you see me, now you don't" routine when he up and retired after a short shelf life (along with his dino brothers Rex and Steg). Bronty is the toughest of the three. The popularity of the dinos after their retirement might mean that Ty will bring them back (in new colors) in the future.
Value: $500.00

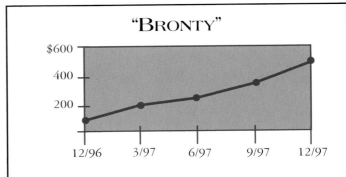

"BUBBLES" THE FISH (R)

Born: 7 - 2 - 95
Released: 1995
Retired: May 1997
Description: Beanie Baby fish aren't all that popular until after they retire. It's not unlike painters who are relatively unknown while alive, only to have their artwork skyrocket in price after they pass away. This yellow and black fish might actually be the best looking of the three BB fish, although you might mix him up with Bumble if you see him from a distance.
Value: $55.00

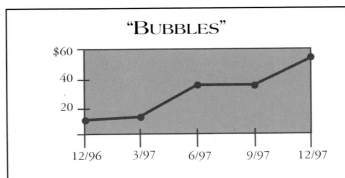

"BUCKY" THE BEAVER (R)

Born: 6 - 8 - 95
Released: 1996
Retired: Dec. 31, 1997
Description: A finely styled Beanie Baby, Bucky has the cuteness to take him a long way in collectors' hearts. He has been produced in ample (but not too large) quantities. His recent retirement has suddenly sparked new interest in this toothy BB.
Value: $20.00

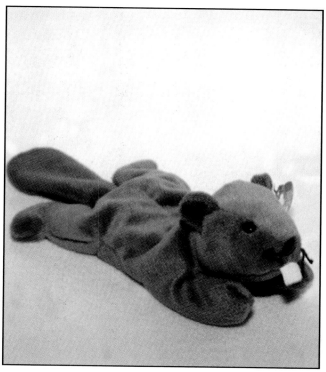

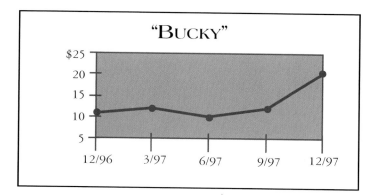

"BUMBLE" THE BEE (R)

Born: N/A
Released: 1995
Retired: 1996
Description: Bumble really made strides in value in 1997, going from $70 at the start of the year to more than $300 by the end. This retired Beanie Baby is certainly not the most outstanding in design, but he makes up for it in his scarcity.
Value: $325.00

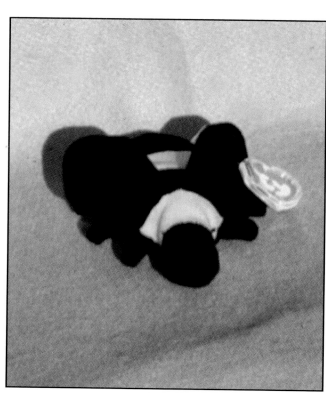

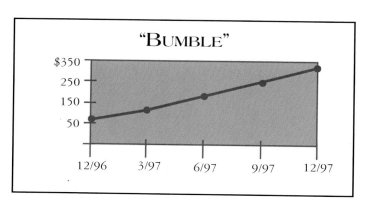

"CAW" THE CROW (R)

Born: N/A
Released: 1995
Retired: 1996
Description: A short-run Beanie Baby, Caw climbed to his current price from about $50 early in 1997. Caw remains a popular style among BB hunters who should keep up enough pressure to force prices upward over the next year.
Value: $350.00

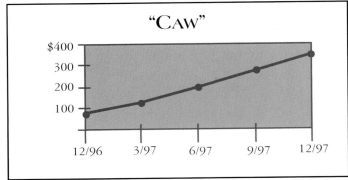

"CHILLY" THE POLAR BEAR (R)

Born: N/A
Released: 1994
Retired: 1995
Description: Collectors warmed up to Chilly almost immediately, but poor Chilly didn't last too long in the Beanie Baby lineup. Since he's white, he shows dirt and wear easily. A mint version of this highly desirable BB is a very tough find. Chilly is a BB that most collectors can only dream about owning, due to his scarcity and high price.
Value: $875.00

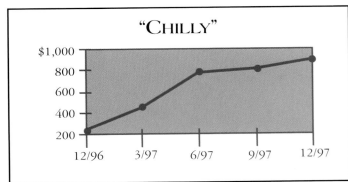

"CHIP" THE CALICO CAT

Born: 1 - 26 - 97
Released: May 1997
Description: Chip joined Nip, Snip, Zip, and Flip to form a formidable fivesome of Beanie Baby cats (Flip and Nip have since gone on to greener pastures). This brown, black, and white kitty is the cutest of the lot in many people's eyes. So far, Chip hasn't been produced in massive quantities, but he hasn't been impossible to find. Like most of the May 1997 releases, he doesn't last long on retailer shelves.
Value: $12.00

"CHOCOLATE" THE MOOSE

Born: 4 - 27 - 93
Released: 1994
Note: Also made as McDonald's Teenie Beanie Baby; one of the "Original 9" BBs
Description: Chocolate, an original Beanie Baby, has been a favorite style of collectors since his release. His rich brown color and bright orange horns are striking. He's been in circulation for quite some time; there should be an ample supply for the near future. However, once retirement sets in, look for a small but good jump in value.
Value: $11.00

"CHOPS" THE LAMB (R)

Born: 5 - 3 - 96
Released: 1996
Retired: January 1997
Note: Also made as McDonald's Teenie Beanie Baby
Description: As far as most collectors are concerned, Chops retired way too soon. One of the more coveted styles, he was replaced by Fleece at the beginning of 1997. Making him even more popular is the fact that he was made into a McDonald's Teenie Beanie Baby, and many collectors want the regular-size Chops to go along with their mini Chops. The future looks pretty bright for Chops.
Value: $80.00

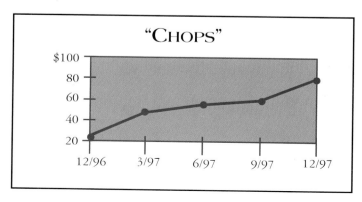

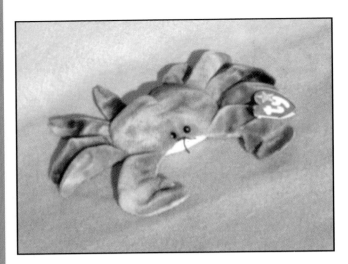

"CLAUDE" THE TIE-DYED CRAB

Born: 9 - 3 - 96
Released: May 1997
Description: All tie-dyed Beanie Babies are especially sought. Claude is no exception. The same style as the retired Digger, Claude has a tie-dyed top and legs, and a cream-colored belly. Claude has very cool tie-dyed colors (unlike some of the other tie-dyed animals).
Value: $12.00

"CONGO" THE GORILLA

Born: 11 - 9 - 96
Released: 1996
Description: A most serious-looking Beanie Baby, Congo almost appears to be the alter-ego to the fun-loving Bongo. Bongo and Congo are often packaged and sold as a pair by dealers. A tough Beanie to get in the summer of 1997, he was out in good numbers by the fall.
Value: $12.00

"CORAL" THE FISH (R)

Born: 3 - 2 - 95
Released: 1995
Retired: January 1997
Description: Coral, a tie-dyed fish, was the first fish to retire. While she is tie-dyed and the other tie-dyed styles have been popular, the same cannot be said for Coral. However, given Coral's still somewhat limited appeal, and the current price, she might well be a little undervalued at this time.
Value: $80.00

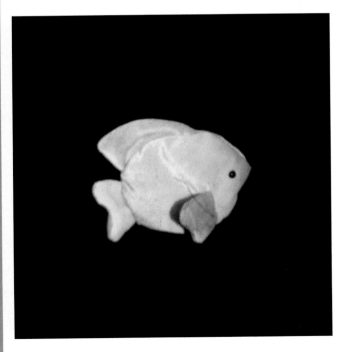

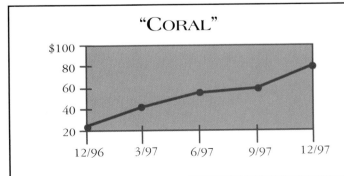

"CRUNCH" THE SHARK

Born: 1 - 13 - 96
Released: January 1997
Description: Poor Crunch is likely the most unloved Beanie Baby in circulation. He's usually the last to be sold in retailer shipments. Comments from collectors are generally along the lines of, "He looks scary." Crunch has been out in good quantities so far; should he be retired soon, his value would change in a hurry. There probably aren't big stashes of Crunch in dealer stocks since he is so unpopular. It's possible that his future value might be higher than more popular styles.
Value: $10.00

"CUBBIE"/"BROWNIE" THE BEAR (R)

Born: 11 - 14 - 96
Released: 1994
Retired: Dec. 31, 1997
Variations: "Cubbie," "Brownie"
Note: One of the "Original 9" BBs
Description: Cubbie, now retired, is the brown version of Blackie. This original Beanie Baby was pretty much out of circulation for most of 1997, but he began appearing on shelves in good quantities again in November, allowing many collectors to fill the "Cubbie" hole in their collection. Cubbie was originally named Brownie. Some early releases (Style 1 hang tags) may be found with "Brownie" hang tag (Brownie looks the same as Cubbie in all regards). Brownie versions are very scarce. On two home-game dates in 1997, the Chicago Cubs gave out Cubbies to the first 10,000 fans under the age of 13 to attend each game. These Cubbies were handed out with a special commemorative certificate. Add $75 to $100 to the price of Cubbie if you own one of these special Cubbies with the certificate.
Value: "Cubbie"—$15.00; "Brownie"—$1,100.00

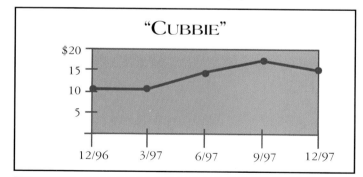

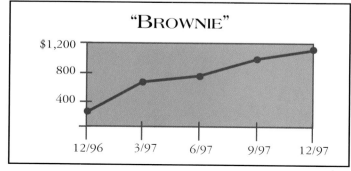

"CURLY" THE BEAR

Born: 4 - 12 - 96
Released: 1996
Description: Curly, along with Teddy the brown bear, were both on the tough-to-find list in 1997. Teddy was retired in September 1997, and has since gone on to be quite valuable. If Ty doesn't release many more of the nappy-haired Curlys in the near future, and if he finds himself retired soon, he'll be in the same money class as Teddy the brown bear. If Ty does release Curly in good numbers again, adjust his current value downward. I spotted Curly on store shelves just twice in 1997—once in April and once in December.
Value: $27.00

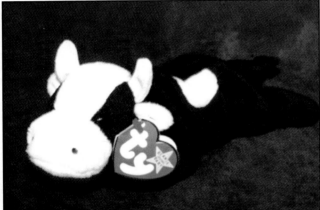

"DAISY" THE COW

Born: 5 - 10 - 94
Released: 1994
Description: After the retirement of Bessie in September 1997, that left just one cow in the Beanie Baby pasture. Daisy is quite popular. Many non-Beanie Baby collectors who have an association with farms and farming want Daisy, as do collectors of cow memorabilia. Daisy has been out in good numbers throughout 1997, but she doesn't stay long on the shelves. Once retirement comes, which could be soon, Daisy's value should be strong.
Value: $10.00

"DERBY" THE HORSE

Born: 9 - 16 - 95
Released: 1995
Variations: diamond (current), coarse mane/plain forhead (possibly discontinued), fine mane (discontinued)
Description: Derby provides evidence of the hard-core nature of some Beanie Baby collectors. Originally issued with a fine mane that was soon changed to a coarse mane, the fine mane version fetches big money today. Such a little difference makes such a big difference! Derby is a nicely-styled horse. His dark brown mane, set against his light brown body, makes him stand out in a crowd of beanies. As this book went to print, there was confirmation of a new Derby variation. The new Derby has a white diamond in the middle of his forehead. This is a great looking variation.
Value: diamond—$11.00; coarse/plain—$11.00; fine mane—$700.00

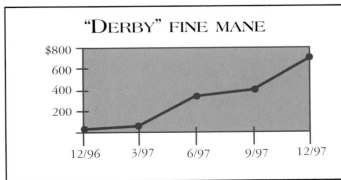

"DERBY" FINE MANE

"DIGGER" THE CRAB (R)

Born: 8 - 23 - 95
Released: 1995
Retired: May 1997
Variations: red, orange
Description: The orange Digger was discontinued in 1995, then replaced by the red version of Digger. The orange Digger is a highly sought and rarely found version, as you can guess from the price. The red Digger is not an extremely hard-to-find Beanie Baby, but you'll still have to spend up to $50 if you want one.
Value: red—$45.00; orange—$375.00

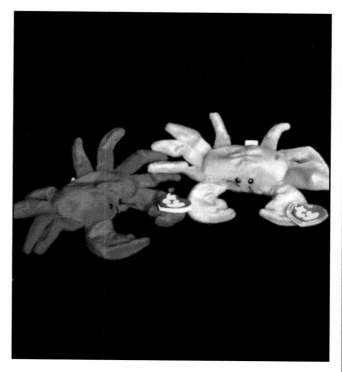

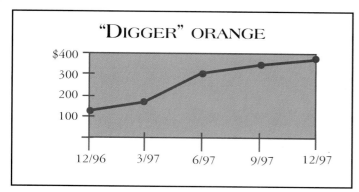

"DIGGER" ORANGE

"DOBY" THE DOBERMAN

Born: 10 - 9 - 96
Released: January 1997
Description: One of the cuter Beanie Baby dogs, Doby doesn't look at all menacing (as real-life Dobermans do). Like most of the current BBs, Doby has been out in strong numbers for most of 1997. Rumors abound that there are too many dogs in the current BB lineup, and that more will be retired soon. Spot was the only dog sent to the kennels in September 1997, so it's possible that more dogs could be retired. Will it be Doby? No one's guess is better than anyone else's. Only Ty knows for sure.
Value: $10.00

"DOODLE" THE ROOSTER (R)

Born: 3 - 8 - 96
Released: May 1997
Retired: July 1997
Description: Doodle caused quite a stir in 1997. First, Doodle received limited distribution, as did the other new May 1997 styles. By the time Doodle began to make his way into stores, it was reported and later confirmed that Doodle's name would be changed to Strut. This was done likely because his name conflicted with the name of a mascot (Doodles) for a restaurant chain (Chick-fil-A). Doodle immediately went from $10 to $100 . . . literally overnight! More Doodles were in the pipeline and eventually the price fell from $100 to about $35 by the fall of 1997. Strut is identical to Doodle except for the name on the tags.
Value: $37.00

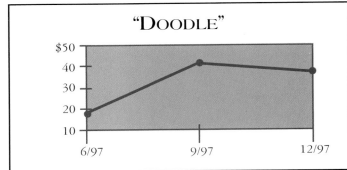

"DOTTY" THE DALMATIAN

Born: 10 - 17 - 96
Released: May 1997
Description: Dotty was a replacement for Sparky, who was retired due to a legal problem with his name. Dotty might have been a second-string Beanie Baby, but collectors still love him all the same. Perhaps his popularity has something to do with Disney's feature-length cartoon and recent live-action film of *101 Dalmatians*. Dotty and Sparky have the same style, but Dotty has black ears and a black tail, while Sparky has white ears and a white tail.
Value: $11.00

"EARS" THE BUNNY

Born: 4 - 18 - 95
Released: 1996
Description: Ears, compared to Hippity, Hoppity, and Floppity, is a very realistic-looking bunny. While he scores well in the cute department, he lacks the charisma of the trio of pastel bunnies. Wouldn't it be great if Ty made a white bunny and/or a black bunny to complement Ears? Strength in numbers counts when it comes to BBs, as can be seen with the popularity of the bunny trio and the many cats.
Value: $10.00

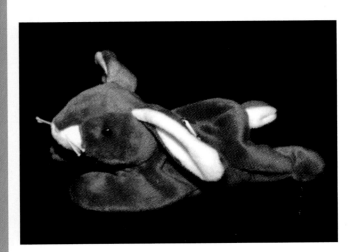

"ECHO" THE DOLPHIN

Born: 12 - 21 - 96
Released: May 1997
Error: Echo with Waves tags
Description: Echo the dolphin and Waves the whale . . . or was that Echo the whale and Waves the dolphin? It was confusing for a time in 1997 as to who was who. Both Echo and Waves were new in May 1997, and their tags were switched. Many of these were released into circulation over the summer and even into the fall season, with both the correct and error versions available at the same time. Because there were so many error versions on the marketplace, there is not a great deal of price difference between the correct and error versions.
Value: $12.00

"FLASH" THE DOLPHIN (R)

Born: 5 - 13 - 93
Released: 1994
Retired: May 1997
Note: One of the "Original 9" BBs
Description: Flash was around for so long that collectors thought he might never leave. But, alas, Flash left the Beanie Baby pool in the May 1997 retirements. After retiring, he was laboring around $30 to $35 for several months, but he climbed to $50 by the end of the year. With new collectors (those who began collecting after May 1997) going back to collect BBs they don't have, expect a good future for Flash.
Value: $50.00

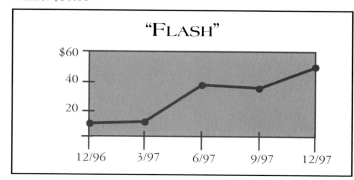

"FLASH"

"FLEECE" THE LAMB

Born: 3 - 21 - 96
Released: January 1997
Description: Like the retired Chops the lamb, Fleece is a collector favorite. Fleece is another Beanie Baby that doesn't linger on store shelves. Cute as a button, wouldn't it be nice if Ty added a black version of Fleece soon? Be careful with Fleece, as his white coat easily picks up and shows dirt, dust, and stains.
Value: $12.00

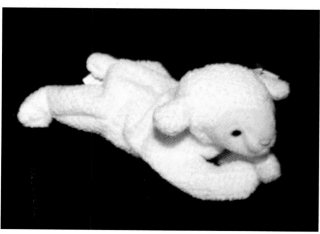

"FLIP" THE CAT (R)

Born: 2 - 28 - 95
Released: 1996
Retired: Sept. 30, 1997
Description: In the summer of 1997, everyone knew that at least one of the three oldest cats (Flip, Nip, or Zip) would be sent packing in the next round of retirements. Of the five cats that were current in 1997, only Snip and Chip were available in any kind of regularity, so it was a good guessing game for collectors as to which kitty was going to go (personally, I bet on Nip). Nip and Zip were the two likeliest since they had been around the longest. But it was Flip who took those final steps from the litter box to the Beanie Baby retirement home. Flip was seen in retailer shipments as late as December 1997.
Value: $32.00

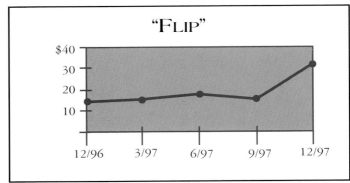

"FLOPPITY" THE BUNNY

Born: 5 - 28 - 96
Released: January 1997
Description: Floppity is the purple component of the pastel bunny trio. Released at the beginning of 1997, these bunnies were considered by collectors to be possible seasonal Beanie Babies (they're perfect for the Easter season). The trio was tough to get in the first half of 1997, but then the floodgates opened and out hopped tons of these bunnies. The secondary market prices fell from $60 for the set to about $40 within a month or two. This trio will always be very popular, no matter how many are produced.
Value: $14.00

"FLUTTER" THE BUTTERFLY (R)

Born: N/A
Released: 1995
Retired: 1996
Description: With her tie-dyed wings and big black body, Flutter is a little bulky looking, if you ask me. Perhaps a brighter center would've cheered her up a bit! Her lack of popularity might have been part of the reason she was retired so quickly. That's also the reason Flutter's valued so highly today.
Value: $525.00

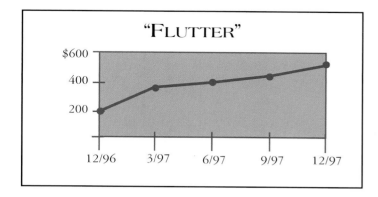

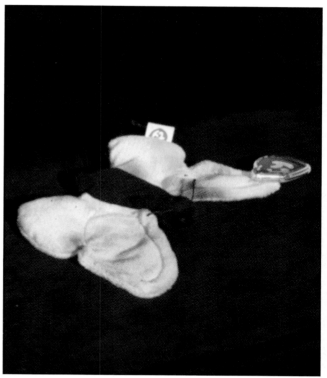

"FRECKLES" THE LEOPARD

Born: 6 - 3 - 96
Released: 1996
Mistakes: Hang tag with birth date 7 - 28 - 96
Description: Freckles was out in decent numbers throughout 1997. Still, as one of the more popular styles, she left the shelves pretty quickly. Freckles is a style that non-Beanie Baby collectors and casual collectors buy because she has such a striking design. She is my personal favorite.
Value: $10.00

"GARCIA" THE BEAR (R)

Born: 8 - 1 - 95
Released: 1996
Retired: May 1997
Description: Is Garcia the most popular Beanie Baby ever? Probably. This tie-dyed teddy, thought to be named in reference to Jerry Garcia (the late lead singer from the Grateful Dead), is wanted by BB collectors and fans of Jerry Garcia and/or tie-dye. When Garcia retired in May 1997, there were a lot of unhappy new collectors who really wanted to get him at the $5 to $10 level. Garcia immediately jumped to about $70, then settled back under $50, only to rebound toward the end of the year.
Value: $75.00

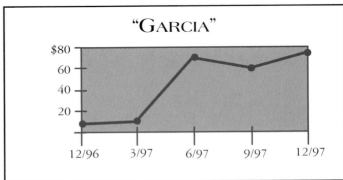

"GOBBLES" THE TURKEY

Born: 11 - 27 - 96
Released: Sept. 30, 1997
Description: Collectors devoured Gobbles as soon as he arrived in stores. Like the other new September 1997 releases, Gobbles is considered a seasonal Beanie Baby who could be retired soon after he's released (within a year). Secondary market prices, in the first month of release, were outrageous ($75 to $150); but if the past is any indication of the future, patience will be rewarded and there should be plenty of Gobbles at retail prices.
Value: $15.00

"GOLDIE" THE FISH (R)

Born: 11 - 14 - 94
Released: 1995
Retired: Dec. 31, 1997
Note: Also made as McDonald's Teenie Beanie Baby
Description: Throughout 1997, almost everyone was certain that Goldie would bite the dust. Goldie finally relinquished, and was retired on the last day of 1997. There were schools of Goldies available throughout most of the year, and it's likely that most every active collector who wants her, has her (thus, her low current value).
Value: $12.00

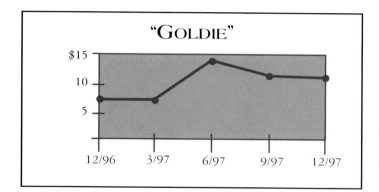

"GRACIE" THE SWAN

Born: 6 - 17 - 96
Released: January 1997
Variations: orange beak/feet (current), fluorescent orange beak/bigger feet (current)
Description: Gracie was another Beanie Baby that people were sure was going to be retired in the next go-around. But Gracie made it through another round of cuts to swim one more day. Collectors noticed that Gracie was given a slightly different-colored beak in about August 1997, changing from orange to fluorescent orange. Her feet also appeared to have been made bigger, too. This slight style change is mildly interesting, but has done nothing in regards to price for either version.
Value: $9.00

"GRUNT" THE RAZORBACK (R)

Born: 7 - 19 - 95
Released: 1996
Retired: May 1997
Description: Grunt, with his deep red coat, is very similar to Snort and Tabasco in color. A very cool Beanie Baby who retired way too early, he's one of the harder to find recent retirees. Don't expect Grunt's value to stay where it is. An upward price movement is very likely in the coming year. Warning: Reports of fake Grunts were out in late 1997. The fake Grunts have wrinkled fabric, poorly cut hang tags, and poor printing on the inside of the hang tags.
Value: $100.00

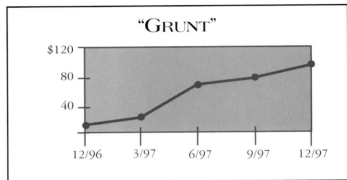

"GRUNT"

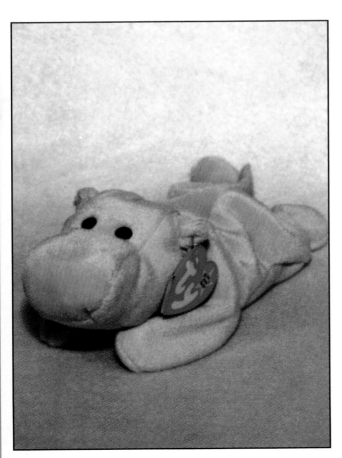

"HAPPY" THE HIPPO

Born: 2 - 25 - 94
Released: 1995
Variations: lavender (current), gray (discontinued)
Description: In a gray version, Happy is highly sought; it was a short-run hippo, retiring sometime in 1995. In lavender, she's not a hot style of Beanie Baby (by any means), but she's not unpopular either. A very simple design and light color is a hindrance that will likely keep Happy from becoming a Beanie Baby classic. How about a tie-dyed hippo named "Hippy" to keep Happy company?
Value: lavender—$10.00; gray—$375.00

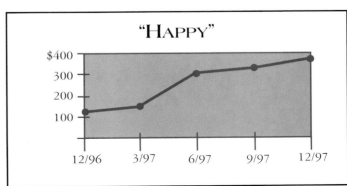

"HAPPY"

"HIPPITY" THE BUNNY

Born: 6 - 1 - 96
Released: January 1997
Description: If you know which bunny is which color, then you're a dedicated Beanie Baby collector. Hippity is the pink third of the bunny triplets. She might be the most pretty BB bunny. I may be biased, however, since Hippity was the first Beanie Baby in my collection and she'll always be very special.
Value: $15.00

"HOOT" THE OWL (R)

Born: 8 - 9 - 95
Released: 1996
Retired: Sept. 30, 1997
Description: If you were in grade school in the 1970s, you probably remember "Woodsy Owl," the bird who implored children to "Give a Hoot. Don't Pollute." Hoot is mindful of Woodsy Owl (however, there was no problem keeping Hoot in the Beanie Baby line because of that). Hoot was one of the BBs on the chopping block and his retirement came in September 1997 to the surprise of few. Hoot is a pretty small and subpar-looking Beanie Baby. With his retirement, he gains in the desirability department, but he's still one of the lowest valued retirees. Collectors wouldn't mind the Hoot style returning, but some brighter colors would be a plus.
Value: $15.00

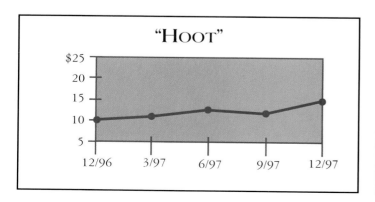

"HOPPITY" THE BUNNY

Born: 4 - 3 - 96
Released: January 1997
Description: Rounding out the bunny threesome is Hoppity, the mint green bunny. There are many rumors that these bunnies will soon be retired and be replaced by three other pastel bunnies. The most often rumored colors are yellow, blue, and orange. But don't rule out a tie-dyed bunny with the name of "Hip-Hop."
Value: $15.00

"HUMPHREY" THE CAMEL (R)

Born: N/A
Released: 1994
Retired: 1995
Description: Humphrey is at or near the top of the wish list of just about every Beanie Baby collector. Few were made and even fewer survived with their tags intact. Humphrey is tough in every sense of the word. BB collectors are wishing Ty would release a new version of Humphrey sometime soon.
Value: $925.00

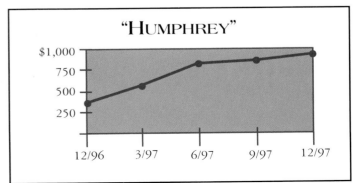

"INCH" THE WORM

Born: 9 - 3 - 95
Released: 1996
Variations: yarn antennae (current), felt antennae (discontinued)
Description: Who says a Beanie Baby worm can't be cute? Many collectors, that's who. Inch falls into the Gracie, Goldie, and Crunch category of "Beanie Babies of lesser popularity." An early felt antennae version is tough, changing over to a yarn antennae within its first year of release. While the felt antennae version is scarce, it's not a really great visual variation, and that fact might be reflected in the price. Collectors aren't willing to spend wads of money on a minor variation.
Value: yarn antennae—$10.00; felt antennae—$90.00

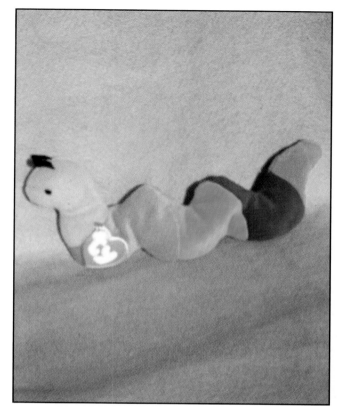

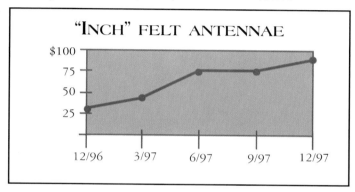

"INKY" THE OCTOPUS

Born: 11 - 29 - 94
Released: 1994
Variations: pink with mouth (current), tan with mouth (discontinued), tan without mouth (discontinued)
Mistakes: There have been reports of pink Inkys without the mouth; however, the stitching could very easily be removed.
Description: One of the stranger looking Beanie Babies, Inky was initially issued in tan: first, without a mouth (with 1st and 2nd style swing tags), and then with a mouth. Each tan variety was available in about equal quantities (which was very few, as you can see by the enormous prices). There are plenty of pink versions on the market. Overall, Inky is not a particular favorite among collectors. Perhaps a name and style change would do him some good: how about Octavius the Octopus?
Value: pink—$12.00; tan w/mouth—$375.00; tan w/o mouth—$425.00

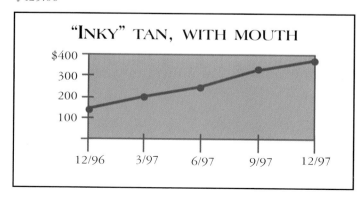

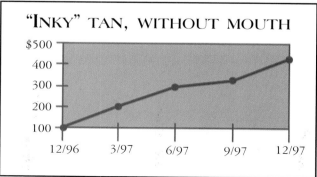

"JOLLY" THE WALRUS

Born: 12 - 2 - 96
Released: May 1997
Description: One criticism of Jolly is that he's a bit on the small-ish side, about the same size as Echo and Waves, two other sea creatures that were also released in May 1997. Other than his size, Jolly is a cutie who looks a lot different from Ty's first walrus, Tusk. Jolly has been available in decent quantities.
Value: $12.00

"KIWI" THE TOUCAN (R)

Born: 9 - 16 - 95
Released: 1995
Retired: January 1997
Description: The colorful Kiwi is one of the brightest Beanie Babies around. And one of the more popular. Not a tough-to-get style, there might be some upward movement in her price as new collectors scramble to buy older retirees.
Value: $90.00

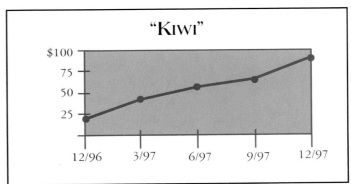

"KIWI"

$100
75
50
25

12/96   3/97   6/97   9/97   12/97

"LEFTY" THE DONKEY (R)

Born: 7 - 4 - 96
Released: 1996
Retired: January 1997
Mistakes: Reports of a missing flag and upside-down flag have surfaced. Be sure to check Lefty carefully if you encounter one of these mistake beanies; it may not be so easy to remove the flag without notice, but removing and re-sewing it upside-down may not be too difficult.
Description: A presidential election year Beanie Baby, Lefty (as well as Righty) was produced for a very short period of time. He has an American flag sewn on his lower back, making him even more appealing. Because of his good styling and short production run, there's little doubt that this outstanding Beanie Baby will continue to escalate in value.
Value: $110.00

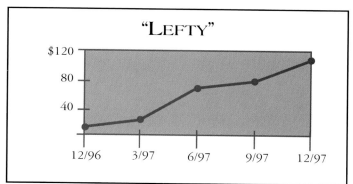

"LEGS" THE FROG (R)

Born: 4 - 25 - 93
Released: 1994
Retired: Sept. 30, 1997
Note: One of the "Original 9" BBs
Description: Legs has been around so long that he might have been a "tadpole" when he was first released. Most collectors agreed that it was time for Legs to "croak." Legs is not "bound" for great "leaps" in value over his present value anytime soon. He was found in decent quantities in 1997, plus he was on the current list for so long that most collectors have at least one Legs in their "pad."
Value: $20.00

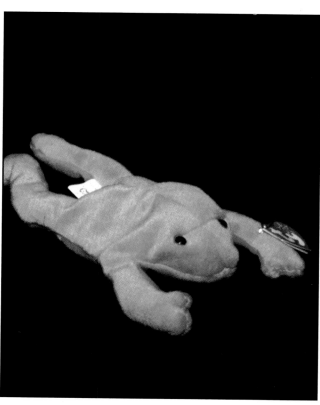

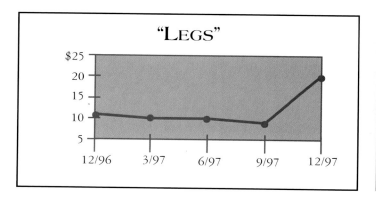

"LIBEARTY" THE BEAR (R)

Born: Summer 1996
Released: 1996
Retired: January 1997
Mistakes: Early beanies produced have tush tags with "Beanie" misspelled as "Beanine." There is no extra value for this minor error. In fact, the error beanie is sometimes worth $10 to $20 less then than the correct beanie! As with Lefty and Righty, beanies with missing or upside-down flags have been reported.
Description: With a U.S. flag stitched over his heart, a birthday in the summer of 1996, and a birthplace of "Atlanta, Georgia, USA," it could be inferred that Libearty was created to celebrate the 1996 Summer Olympics held in Atlanta. It seemed that Libearty lasted about as long as the Olympics. An early retirement made him a particularly expensive and desirable Beanie Baby. The fact that he's a bear is also in his favor. As with all white BBs, keep the dust off this little bear.
Value: $120.00

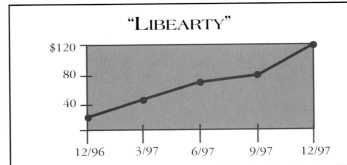

"LIZZY" THE LIZARD (R)

Born: 5 - 11 - 95
Released: 1995
Retired: Dec. 31, 1997
Variations: blue, tie-dyed
Note: Also made as McDonald's Teenie Beanie Baby
Description: One of the longer Beanies, Lizzy measures some 13 inches from the tip of her tongue to the tip of her tail. Lizzy was originally released as a tie-dyed lizard, and that version is very scarce. Valued at around $200 in early 1997, the tie-dyed version has more than doubled in value. How much farther can the tie-dyed Lizzy go? Scarcity may be the key. The blue Lizzy has been readily available since the tie-dyed version bid adieu, but retirement will enhance this item in terms of value and popularity.
Value: blue—$13.00; tie-dyed—$475.00

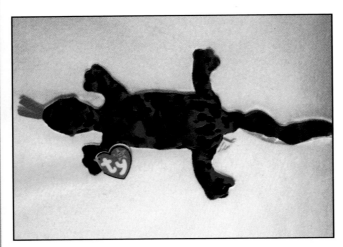

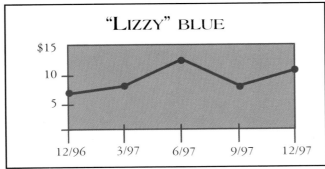

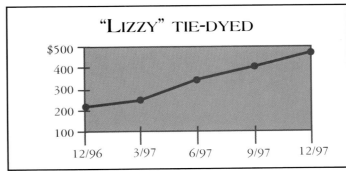

"Lucky" the ladybug

Born: 5 - 1 - 95
Released: 1994
Variations: 11 printed spots (current), 21 printed spots (discontinued), 7 felt spots (discontinued)
Description: There are variations aplenty with Lucky. First issued with seven felt spots that were glued on, that was soon changed because the spots could be removed and they presented a possible hazard to young'uns. Next came Lucky, with 21 small spots. This is a neat looking variation that was produced for a very, very short time. Then came Lucky, with 11 spots, which is how she's currently being produced. There are some variations with the large-spot version, as the number of spots can range from seven to 11 spots. However, there is no price difference.
Value: 11 spots—$9.00; 21 spots—$375.00; 7 felt spots—$95.00

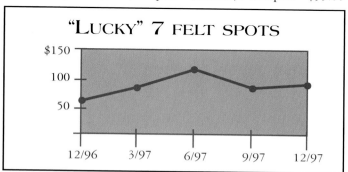

"LUCKY" 7 FELT SPOTS

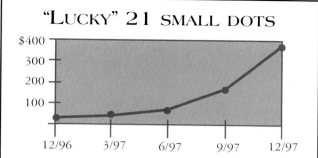

"LUCKY" 21 SMALL DOTS

"Magic" the dragon (R)

Born: 9 - 5 - 95
Released: 1995
Retired: Dec. 31, 1997
Variations: light pink thread on wings; hot pink thread on wings
Description: Magic was an oft-mentioned Beanie Baby retiree (due to the belief that the iridescent pink wings are too expensive for Ty to produce). Retirement day finally came for this mystical creature at the end of 1997. By far one of the most cherished styles Ty ever produced, Magic was available in good quantities throughout 1997. Despite the large production, she continues to draw good prices on the secondary market after her retirement.
Value: light pink thread—$20.00; hot pink thread—$50.00

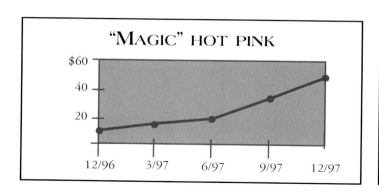

"MAGIC" HOT PINK

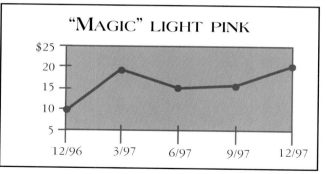

"MAGIC" LIGHT PINK

"MANNY" THE MANATEE (R)

Born: 6 - 8 - 95
Released: 1996
Retired: May 1997
Description: Manny was not very popular when he was issued in 1996. He was a little gray and lifeless looking, perhaps causing his early retirement. Despite his lack of personality, he has scored well on the retired circuit.
Value: $100.00

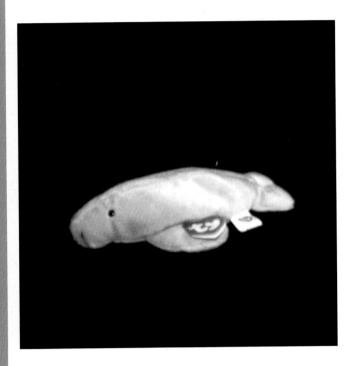

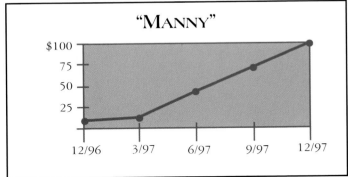

"MAPLE" THE CANADIAN BEAR

Born: 7 - 1 - 96
Released: January 1997
Variations: "Maple" tush tag (current), "Pride" tush tag (discontinued)
Description: The Canada-issued white bear with a Canada flag over his heart has driven U.S. collectors crazy. Available only north of the border, it's been very tough for U.S. collectors to get their hands on (at least at a reasonable price). Many collectors have even crossed the border to try to get the elusive Maple. Maple was first issued with a "Pride" tush tag. These error-tagged Prides are expensive. Your best bet to get a Maple near retail price is by ordering from a Canadian retail outlet (the number of people on waiting lists for Maple is incredibly long) or by having a Canadian friend or relative get you one.
Value: "Maple" tags—$90.00; "Pride" tush tag—$350.00

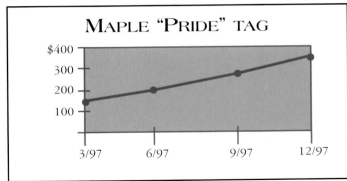

"MEL" THE KOALA

Born: 1 - 15 - 96
Released: January 1997
Description: Mel is in the middle-range of popularity in the Beanie Baby kingdom. Rumors about this little guy surround famed movie star Mel Gibson, touting that Mel the koala was named after Mel Gibson. If this were true, wouldn't Mel the koala be a little cuter?
Value: $10.00

"MYSTIC" THE UNICORN

Born: 5 - 21 - 94
Released: 1994
Variations: coarse mane/iridescent horn (current), coarse mane/gold horn (possibly discontinued), fine mane (discontinued)
Description: Mystic was another oft-mentioned near-future retiree, along with Magic. But Mystic survived the last round of cuts in December 1997. Mystic is one of the most popular styles of BBs produced by Ty. And, Ty has seemingly produced its fair share of Mystics. It appears that there have been more Mystics with a gold horn around in 1997 than almost any other style. Currently issued with a coarse mane, this unicorn was originally given a fine mane (the same type of variation as Derby); the fine-mane version was in circulation for about a year, and today it commands a premium price. In November, Mystic with an iridescent horn was released. If this turns out to be a widely distributed and permanent variation, the secondary market price should be in the $15 to $20 range for a few months, then settle to under $12. However, if this is a short-run variation, or if Mystic is retired soon, look for prices to skyrocket to $50 or more. With the change in horns, the old-horn version (gold) was drawing more interest, and the price moved ahead. However, remember how many of these Mystic versions you saw in 1997 before you pay a premium for one.
Value: coarse mane/iridescent horn—$20; coarse mane/gold horn—$15; fine mane—$155.00

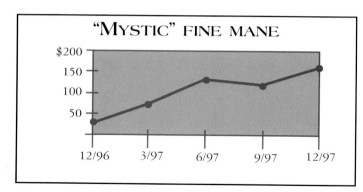

"NANOOK" THE HUSKY

Born: 11 - 21 - 96
Released: May 1997
Description: Nanook might just be the best Beanie Baby dog around. This husky's colors are great, its style is great, and it's little wonder that he's quickly become a BB favorite. Distribution of Nanook has been on the light side in 1997, so he's currently commanding a slightly higher price than some of the other May 1997 releases.
Value: $14.00

"NIP" THE CAT (R)

Born: 3 - 6 - 94
Released: 1995
Retired: Dec. 31, 1997
Variations: gold belly and white paws/whiskers/ears; all gold body, pink ears, and pink whiskers; white belly/face and pink ears/whiskers
Description: Nip and Zip have some of the best variations of any Beanie Babies. The first Nip had a white face and belly, pink ears and whiskers, and the rest of him was gold. The second (and harder-to-get version) had an all-gold body with pink ears. The first two versions were discontinued in 1995. The most recent version has white paws, ears, and whiskers, and the rest of him is gold. Nip is truly adorable, which is one of the reasons why the variations are so highly prized. The most recent version was in short supply most of 1997, but he showed up in very large quantities late in the year, which accounts for his modest value after retirement.
Value: gold belly/white paws—$13.00; all gold—$675.00; white belly—$300.00

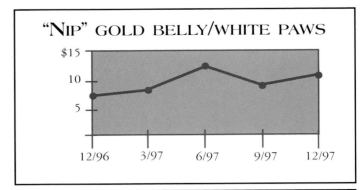

"NIP" GOLD BELLY/WHITE PAWS

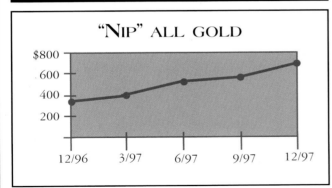

"NIP" ALL GOLD

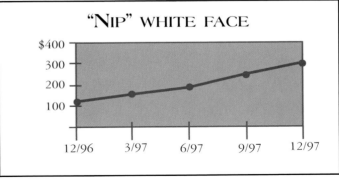

"NIP" WHITE FACE

"Nuts" the Squirrel

Born: 1 - 21 - 96
Released: January 1997
Description: Nuts has about the same appeal as does Mel, which is middle of the road. Nuts has been out in good numbers in 1997. Could a color change help this little fella? Definitely! How about black, red, gray, or white? Those are four other colors that real squirrels can be found in.
Value: $9.00

"Patti" the Platypus

Born: 1 - 6 - 93
Released: 1994
Variations: violet (current), deep magenta (discontinued)
Note: Also made as McDonald's Teenie Beanie Baby; one of the "Original 9" BBs
Description: As one of the original Beanie Babies, Patti will always hold a special place in collectors' hearts. When initially released, Patti was a deep magenta color; this is a very difficult version to locate in mint condition (or any condition, for that matter). Some collectors prefer to recognize three different "darker" version Pattis. While there may be slight differences among deeper color Pattis, all are worth about the same. The current Patti is a lighter violet color. Patti should always remain extremely desirable because of her styling and stand-out color.
Value: violet—$13.00; deep magenta—$650.00

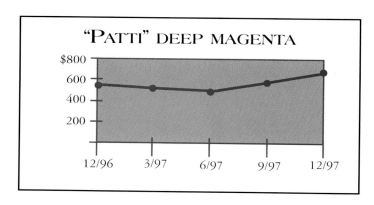

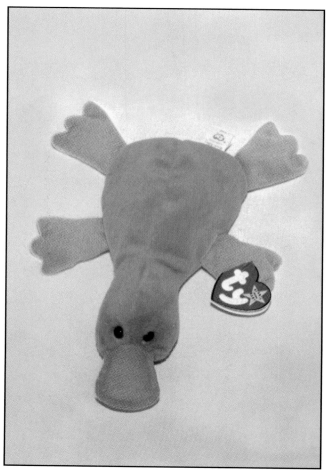

"PEACE" THE TIE-DYED BEAR

Born: 2 - 1 - 96
Released: May 1997
Description: Along with Princess and Doodle, Peace was the most talked-about Beanie Baby in 1997. Following on the success of Garcia, Peace is actually Garcia with the addition of an embroidered "peace symbol" over his heart. While the other newly released May 1997 BBs were hitting the store shelves, Peace was almost nowhere to be found. When he was found, collectors were paying up to $250 for him. As the year went along, that price dropped to its current level as more Peace bears made their way onto retailer shelves. Still, as of the end of 1997, Peace is still a hot current Beanie Baby. Why? Many people want Peace because he's a great go-along with Garcia (and he's so darn hard to get).
Value: $35.00

"PEANUT" THE ELEPHANT

Born: 1 - 25 - 95
Released: 1995
Variations: light blue (current), dark blue (discontinued)
Description: The dark blue Peanut was out for a very, very short period of time in 1995 (with a Style 3 hang tag). He was quickly changed to light blue, which is the current variation. The dark blue Peanut might be the shortest produced Beanie Baby ever, and his price reflects that fact. Herds of the light blue Peanut were out in 1997. An extremely popular style, it shouldn't be long before Peanut calls it a career. Even with the great numbers made, he will be a popular retired BB, whenever that day comes.
Value: light blue—$10.00; dark blue—$1,900.00

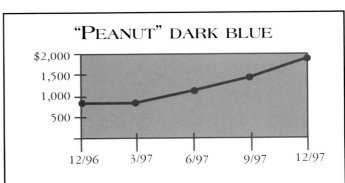

"PEKING" THE PANDA BEAR (R)

Born: N/A
Released: 1994
Retired: 1995
Description: Peking is one of the best-loved Beanie Babies, partly because of his high price, and partly because he's a panda bear. Cute as a button, his value is such that he's out of reach of most collectors. Very difficult to find in top condition with all tags in place.
Value: $825.00

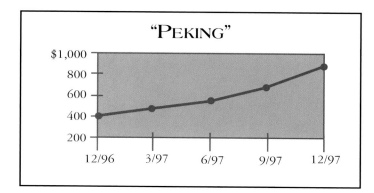

"PINCHERS" THE LOBSTER

Born: 6 - 19 - 93
Released: 1994
Note: one of the "Original 9" BBs
Variations: "Pinchers" hang tag (current), "Punchers" hang tag (discontinued)
Description: This original Beanie Baby was first called Punchers; however, this version (with Style 1 hang tags that say "Punchers" on them) was released on some early examples. These are very pricey, especially considering that the Punchers version is exactly the same as the current Pinchers. Pinchers was just about everywhere in 1997. Everyone who wanted a Pinchers probably has one, as he's a quite common crustacean.
Value: "Pinchers" tag—$12.00; "Punchers" tag—$1125.00

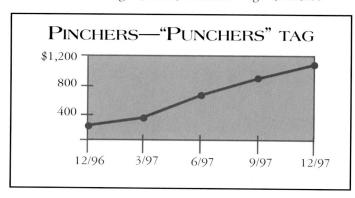

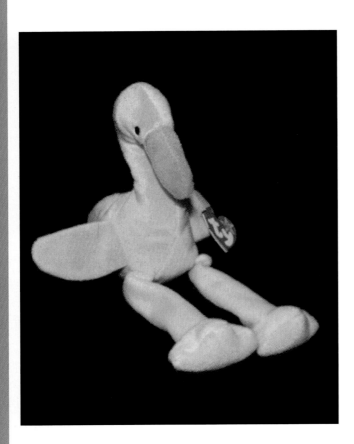

"PINKY" THE FLAMINGO

Born: 2 - 13 - 95
Released: 1995
Note: Also made as McDonald's Teenie Beanie Baby
Description: Pinky gained Beanie Baby fame when she became a Teenie Beanie Baby at McDonald's. Collector interest in this relatively old BB was rekindled. Pinky has been around in good quantities in 1997. She's a favorite of children (and adults who have a pink flamingo or two in their front yard). Watch out for red Pinkys that might be offered for sale. These red versions of Pinky were reportedly purchased in China (along with a lot of other BBs of dubious lineage). It isn't certain if this is a real Beanie Baby variation or a fake. At this time, the likelihood is that it is a fake.
Value: $12.00

"POUCH" THE KANGAROO

Born: 11 - 6 - 96
Released: January 1997
Description: There was one change with this marsupial Beanie Baby in 1997. The baby Pouch inside Momma Pouch's pouch was rumored to be a choking hazard for little children. You could actually remove the baby kangaroo from the pouch, only to find that it was a head only, not an entire baby Kangaroo. Many thought that Ty would redesign or retire Pouch because of this. Pouch is now made with the baby kangaroo attached inside the pouch so it can't be easily pulled out. In either design, Pouch is a very popular Beanie Baby.
Value: $10.00

"PUGSLY" THE PUG DOG

Born: 5 - 2 - 96

Released: May 1997

Description: Pugsly is one of the most popular Beanie Baby dogs. Released in May 1997, he has been out in better numbers than many of the other new releases. He should be popular for years to come. Most collectors expect more dogs to be retired soon. Pugsly isn't one that collectors think will go, but, if he did, his value would be quite high.

Value: $14.00

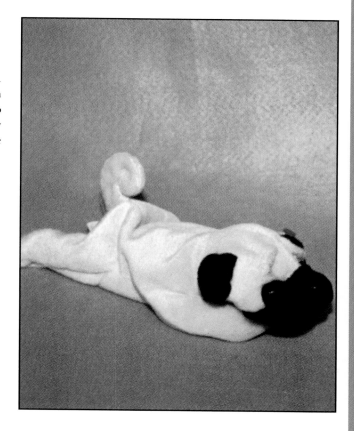

"QUACKERS" THE DUCK

Born: 4 - 19 - 94

Released: 1995

Variations: "Quackers" with wings (current); with "Quacker" tag and wingless (discontinued)

Note: Also made as McDonald's Teenie Beanie Baby

Description: The first issue of Quackers saw his name spelled "Quacker" and he had no wings (some early "Quackers" were also issued sans wings). Poor Quackers looked pretty pathetic without wings, so Ty gave him a set of wings. He looks a whole lot happier now. The wingless variety of this style is rare and highly sought. However, there have been reports of winged Quackers having their wings removed to fool people into thinking they're getting a rare variation, so watch out! There were flocks of the winged Quackers available throughout 1997.

Value: "Quackers" with wings—$8.00; "Quacker" wingless— $1,225.00

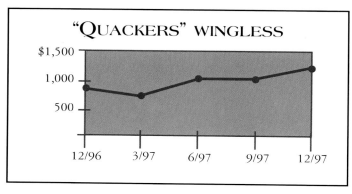

"RADAR" THE BAT (R)

Born: 10 - 30 - 95
Released: 1995
Retired: May 1997
Description: Red-eyed Radar is a Beanie Baby that you either love or hate. Bats have a tendency to do that to people. Radar could be legitimately considered as scary looking. That fact makes him perfect for the Halloween season. Holiday-themed Beanie Babies are usually better sellers, because non-Beanie Baby collectors whose collections are based on the holidays often collect things like Beanie Baby bats. This added pressure has helped Radar maintain his value.
Value: $80.00

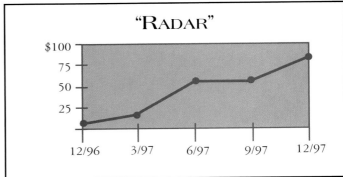

"REX" THE TYRANNOSAURUS (R)

Born: N/A
Released: 1995
Retired: 1996
Description: Rex is the most plentiful of the dinosaur trio that saw time on retailer shelves in 1995 and 1996. But "most plentiful" doesn't translate into "easy to find." This tyrannosaurus rex Beanie Baby is highly sought and uncommon.
Value: $350.00

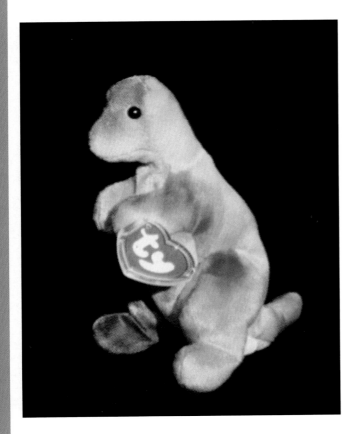

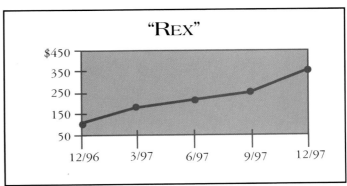

"RIGHTY" THE ELEPHANT (R)

Born: 7 - 4 - 96
Released: 1996
Retired: January 1997
Mistakes: As with Lefty and Libearty, there are reports of a missing flag, and an upside-down flag, on Righty.
Description: Along with Lefty, Righty was a presidential election year Beanie Baby that was made for a brief time. Not quite as visually appealing as Lefty, the gray Righty sports an American flag sewn on his lower back. Both Lefty and Righty are certain winners for the future.
Value: $110.00

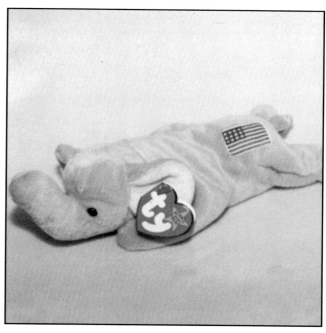

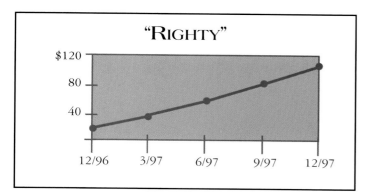

"RINGO" THE RACCOON

Born: 7 - 14 - 95
Released: 1996
Description: Ringo has solid styling for a raccoon Beanie Baby. He was produced in good numbers in 1997, so he shouldn't be one of the real expensive BBs when he retires (which could be anytime soon).
Value: $10.00

"ROARY" THE LION

Born: 2 - 20 - 96
Released: May 1997
Description: Of all May 1997 releases, Roary has been available in the greatest numbers. Even so, the lion style is particularly popular among youngsters, probably due to the association with Disney's *Lion King* movie. I predict that Ty will produce a mate for Roary in the future.
Value: $12.00

"ROVER" THE DOG

Born: 5 - 30 - 96
Released: 1996
Description: Rover, the red Beanie Baby dog, is an adored style. He is cartoonish, in the same way that Bones is cartoonish. He reminds children (and adults) of Clifford the dog, a character featured in many children's books. In fact, I overheard one child exclaim when she saw Rover, "Look, it's Clifford!" In reality, the only thing Rover and Clifford have in common is their color.
Value: $10.00

"SCOOP" THE PELICAN

Born: 7 - 1 - 96
Released: 1996
Description: Collectors grabbed up Scoops throughout 1997. A hard-to-find example early in the year, he was out in good numbers over the last five months of the year. Even though there were many Scoops to be had, he vanished from retailer shelves at a quick rate. His huge orange bill makes Scoop very distinctive.
Value: $10.00

"SCOTTIE" THE DOG

Born: 6 - 15 - 96
Released: 1996
Mistakes: Hang tag with birth date of 6 - 3 - 96
Description: Similar in style to Tuffy (Tuffy has bigger ears), Scottie is an all-black dog. He's pretty cute, but it's difficult to see his face because it's so dark. Expect Ty to retire several dogs over the next year. Scottie could be one of them.
Value: $10.00

"SEAMORE" THE SEAL (R)

Born: 12 - 14 - 96
Released: 1994
Retired: Sept. 30, 1997
Note: Also made as McDonald's Teenie Beanie Baby
Description: For a couple of months preceding the September 1997 retirements, there were rumblings in the Beanie Baby community that Seamore was on his way out. Prices on the secondary market surged as few new shipments made their way onto store shelves. The rumors of Seamore's exit proved true. This little white seal is very cute, and he is one of the most desirable of the September 1997 retirees.
Value: $60.00

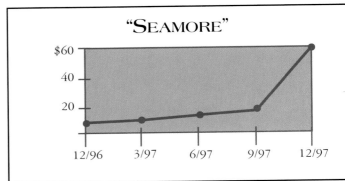

"SEAWEED" THE OTTER

Born: 3 - 19 - 96
Released: 1996
Description: Poor Seaweed! More than once I've heard people say, "What kind of a bear is this?" Obviously, not the greatest designed Beanie Baby, Seaweed could use some restyling. His main problem seems to be that he's too short and stocky. There was an ample supply, but not an overabundance, of Seaweeds out in 1997.
Value: $12.00

"SLITHER" THE SNAKE (R)

Born: N/A
Released: 1994
Retired: 1995
Description: Almost as long as two foot-long hot-dogs, Slither slinked into the Beanie Baby family and slinked right out. A short-run BB, he has similar material as fellow reptiles Speedy and Ally. Like all BBs that were retired more than two years ago, he is hard to find with his tags still intact (yes, people actually bought BBs and gave them to their children to play with).
Value: $775.00

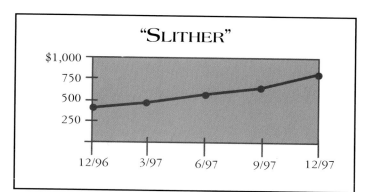

"SLY" THE FOX

Born: 9 - 12 - 96
Released: 1996
Variations: white belly (current), brown belly (discontinued)
Description: Many Beanies Babies changed style not long after introduction. That's what happened to Sly. In his first life, he had an all-brown body. Not long after, his belly was changed to white. The all-brown version is highly coveted. As a style, in either the all-brown or white-belly version, Sly is one of the most liked BBs.
Value: white belly—$11.00; brown belly—$90.00

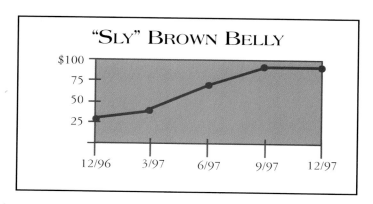

"SNIP" THE CAT

Born: 10 - 22 - 96
Released: January 1997
Description: This Siamese cat was another fine domestic cat added to the Beanie Baby line. As popular as the other cats, Snip was widely available through most of 1997. He's a favorite of cat lovers and children.
Value: $10.00

"SNORT" THE BULL

Born: 5 - 15 - 95
Released: January 1997
Mistake: There are Snorts with Tabasco tags. Add $10 to $20 for this error.
Note: Also made as McDonald's Teenie Beanie Baby
Description: Snort was a replacement for Tabasco. The difference between the two bulls is the feet. Tabasco has red feet, and Snort has white feet. The Snort/Tabasco style is likely in the top 10 all-time favorite Beanie Baby styles. Snort has been largely obtainable throughout 1997.
Value: $10.00

"SNOWBALL" THE SNOWMAN (R)

Born: 12 - 22 - 96
Released: Sept. 30, 1997
Retired: Dec. 31, 1997
Description: Adding to its line of non-real animal Beanie Babies (Spooky, Mystic, and Magic), Ty introduced a snowman. Like all new releases, Snowball bagged monster dollars in the first few weeks after he became available. As more of these snowmen were released, the price melted. However, an abrupt retirement (a la 1997 Teddy) has pumped new life into this cold BB. Is there any chance of a Snow Woman to follow?
Value: $20.00

(No value chart is presented for this retired item due to its brief three-month production period.)

"SPARKY" THE DALMATIAN (R)

Born: 2 - 27 - 96
Released: 1996
Retired: May 1997
Description: "Sparky the Fire Dog," is a registered trademark of the National Fire Protection Association. This may be the reason Sparky was retired not long after his release. Sparky was replaced by Dotty. Many Sparkys made their way into collectors' hands, so Sparky is not rare, but he is still desirable. The difference between Sparky and Dotty is that Sparky has white ears and a white tail, while Dotty has black ears and a black tail.
Value: $55.00

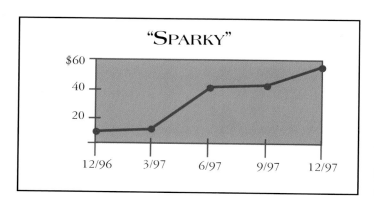

"SPEEDY" THE TURTLE (R)

Born: 8 - 14 - 94
Released: 1994
Retired: Sept. 30, 1997
Note: Also made as McDonald's Teenie Beanie Baby
Description: A not-so-popular style of Beanie Baby, Speedy was one that people predicted would soon be retired. And they were right. Speedy was retired in September 1997. He is one of the least popular newly retirees (along with Legs and Hoot), and that fact is reflected in his price. He was also available in great quantities in 1997.
Value: $22.00

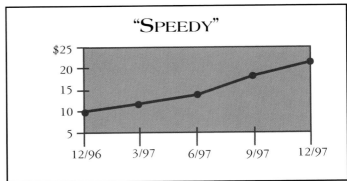

"SPIKE" THE RHINO

Born: 8 - 13 - 96
Released: 1996
Description: Spike was one of the tough-to-get Beanie Babies in 1997. I saw him just four times, but he did start trickling into stores again in late November 1997; if this trickle turns into a gush (like what happened to Nip and Zip), look for his price to drop. If there aren't many issued, and Ty retires him soon, look for him to follow Tank in value.
Value: $21.00

"SPINNER" THE SPIDER

Born: 10 - 28 - 96
Released: Sept. 30, 1997
Description: Thought to be a seasonal (Halloween) Beanie Baby, Spinner is a highly popular and creepy style. Early prices were high—$50 or more. Like the other new releases, exercise patience and get your Spinner for $5 to $10 later on.
Value: $23.00

"SPLASH" THE WHALE (R)

Born: 7 - 8 - 93
Released: 1994
Retired: May 1997
Note: One of the "Original 9" BBs
Description: An original Beanie Baby, Splash has always been a popular style. Look for this orca whale to have the same bright future as Flash, another original BB who was retired the same time as Splash. Splash is a much neater style than Waves, the orca-style whale that replaced Splash.
Value: $50.00

"SPLASH"

$60				
40				
20				
12/96	3/97	6/97	9/97	12/97

"SPOOKY" THE GHOST (R)

Born: 10 - 31 - 95
Released: 1995
Retired: Dec. 31, 1997
Variations: "Spooky" tag; "Spook" tag
Description: One of the top five most-wanted Beanie Babies, Spooky was originally issued with "Spook" tags. These Spook varieties are scarce. Spooky was out in decent numbers for a couple of months in the summer of 1997, but he all but disappeared from shipments for most of 1997, and now he's retired (did he vanish into thin air . . . like a ghost?). It's likely that because so many non-Beanie Baby collectors want Spooky, his value will continue to rise.
Value: "Spooky" tag—$25.00; "Spook" tag—$150.00

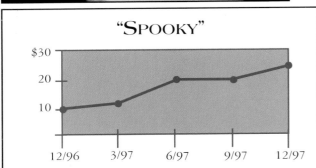

"SPOT" THE DOG (R)

Born: 1 - 3 - 93
Released: 1994
Retired: Sept. 30, 1997
Note: One of the "Original 9" BBs
Variations: with spot, without spot (both retired)
Description: Spot has one of the most famous variations of any Beanie Baby. He was first issued without a spot on his back. A spot was added in 1994, and the Spot version without a spot is highly rare and expensive. A Beanie Baby original, he was retired in September 1997, and has since proven to be a popular retiree. Spot was not plentiful during 1997, but he was not too hard to find either. In fact, some stores had Spot up to a month after his retirement. There have been reports of fake Spots without a spot. Watch out!
Value: with a spot—$25.00; without a spot—$1,250.00

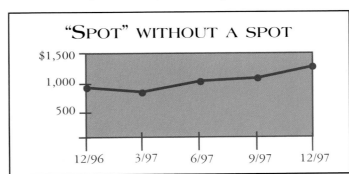

"SQUEALER" THE PIG

Born: 4 - 23 - 93
Released: 1994
Note: One of the "Original 9" BBs
Description: Farm animal-related Beanie Babies have always been a popular style, be they Bessie, Daisy, Chops, Strut or Snort. Squealer is no exception. This light-pink pig is just about perfect, which might be the reason he's been in the BB stable since the beginning. Many Squealers were in stores in 1997, and he was one of the BBs who left the shelves quite quickly. The end of the line can't be far for Squealer, as more of the original BBs are retired.
Value: $10.00

"STEG" THE STEGOSAURUS (R)

Born: N/A
Released: 1995
Retired: 1996
Description: Most Stegs have a tie-dyed green-brown color, which is not the most attractive. However, Steg's high scarcity level makes him highly valuable and immensely more attractive.
Value: $400.00

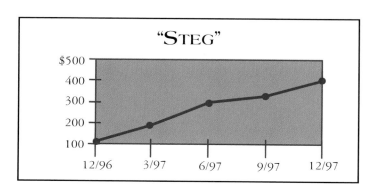

"STEG"

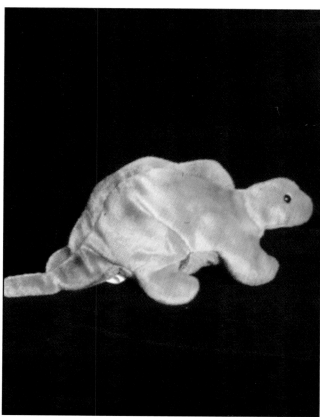

"STING" THE RAY (R)

Born: 8 - 27 - 95
Released: 1995
Retired: January 1997
Description: Some say Sting's a manta ray, other say he's a stingray. Well, you can call him anything, but don't call him current. This tie-dyed sea creature retired more than a year ago, and he has gained fans since then. Sting has a neat style that most collectors would love to see return.
Value: $85.00

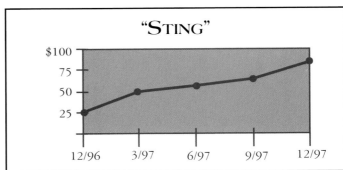

"STINKY" THE SKUNK

Born: 2 - 13 - 95
Released: 1995
Description: You couldn't ask for a much worse name for such a finely styled Beanie Baby. Stinky does anything but stink when it comes to his appearance. Almost graceful, this black and white skunk is a true favorite, especially when kids see him. He's been current for a long stretch, but there are other BBs more deserving of a retirement than Stinky. Wouldn't a pink and white female skunk be a great Beanie Baby? Too bad the name "Pinky" is already taken. We could have had Stinky and Pinky the skunk duo!
Value: $11.00

"STRIPES" THE TIGER

Born: 6 - 11 - 95
Released: 1995
Variations: tan/black (current), orange/black with fuzzy belly (discontinued), orange/black (discontinued)
Description: Stripes proves that a tiger can change its stripes and color and still remain on the top. One of the best-loved Beanie Babies, Stripes was originally issued in an orange color with more black stripes; this version was out for just a short period of time. There was also the orange/black version with a very fuzzy belly in very short availability. The current Stripes has fewer stripes and is a lighter tan color. Stripes is getting a bit long in the tooth, and it shouldn't be too much longer before he retires. Plenty of Stripes were available in 1997, so there should be an ample supply down the road.
Value: tan/black—$10.00; orange/black with fuzzy belly—$425.00; orange/black—$225.00

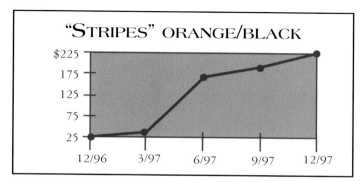

"STRIPES" ORANGE/BLACK

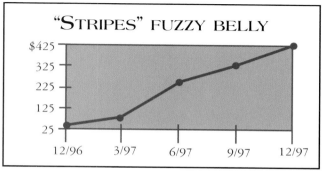

"STRIPES" FUZZY BELLY

"STRUT" THE ROOSTER

Born: 3 - 8 - 96
Released: August 1997
Description: This rooster came along as a replacement for Doodle in August 1997. Strut is identical to Doodle except for the name on the tags.
Value: $18.00

"TABASCO" THE BULL (R)

Born: 5 - 15 - 95
Released: 1995
Retired: January 1997
Description: Due to a conflict with his name, Tabasco was retired. An extremely popular style, Tabasco is almost an icon for Beanie Babies. He was replaced by Snort upon retirement (Tabasco has red feet and Snort has white feet). Tabasco is popular on the secondary market, as you can see by his value. His high price is not because he is scarce or rare (he might be best described as uncommon); his value rests more in his popularity.
Value: $150.00

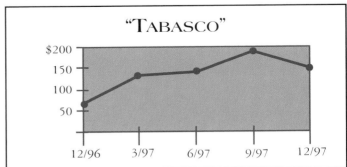

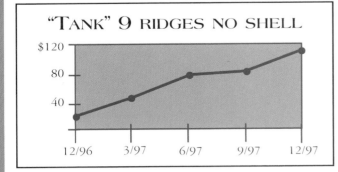

"TANK" THE ARMADILLO (R)

Born: 2 - 22 - 95
Released: 1996
Retired: Sept. 30, 1997
Variations: 9 ridges with shell; 7 ridges, no shell; 9 ridges, no shell
Description: In his lifetime, Tank went through a metamorphosis. He started his life with no shell, and seven or nine ridges on his back (these varieties were produced in about equal numbers), and he looked more like an aardvark than an armadillo. These versions were retired in 1996. The new Tank was fitted properly—with a shell and nine ridges, and he lost his longer aardvark appearance. Tank was just about non-existent in 1997. I saw him just once. Along with Teddy and Seamore, Tank is the most desired September 1997 retiree.
Value: 9 ridges with shell—$50.00; 7 ridges, no shell—$100.00; 9 ridges, no shell—$110.00

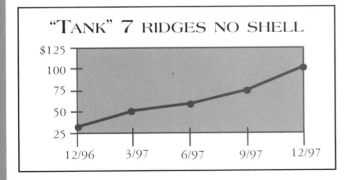

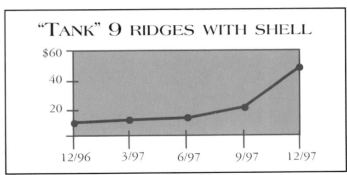

"TEDDY" THE BEAR (R)

Born: 11 - 28 - 95 (new face brown bear is the only Teddy with a birth date)

Released: 1994 (old-faced bears), 1995 (new-faced bears)

Retired: 1995 (all but Teddy, the new face brown bear)
Sept. 30, 1997—Teddy the new face brown bear

Variations: brown new face, cranberry new face, jade new face, magenta new face, teal new face, violet new face, brown old face, cranberry old face, jade old face, magenta old face, teal old face, violet old face

Note: the original face ("old-faced" bears) have thin and long faces. The "new-faced" bears have fuller, rounded faces.

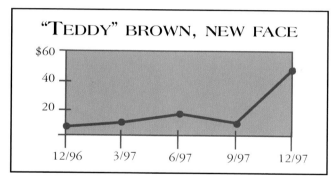

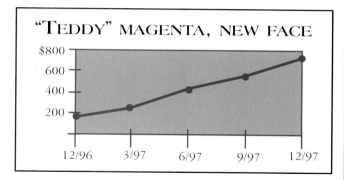

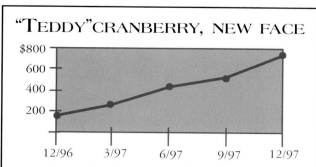

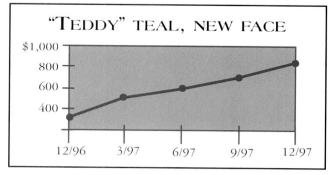

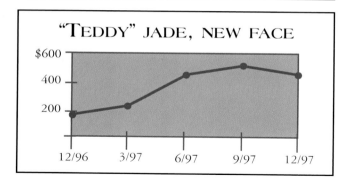

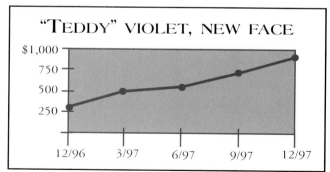

"TEDDY" THE BEAR (CONTINUED)

Description: With the retirement of Teddy the brown bear, new-face version, the colorful Teddy chapter has seemingly come to an end. The original six Teddys, in their cool colors and new and old faces, are some of the most valuable of all Beanie Babies. The one exception is the new-face Teddy the brown bear, who was retired in September 1997. The others were retired in 1995. The old-face brown bear is considered the toughest to find of any of the 12 different varieties.

Value: brown new face—$50.00; brown old face—$1,000.00
cranberry new face—$750.00; cranberry old face—$800.00
jade new face—$450.00; jade old face—$675.00
magenta new face—$750.00; magenta old face—$675.00
teal new face—$825.00; teal old face—$750.00
violet new face—$900.00; violet old face—$675.00

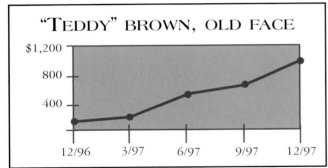

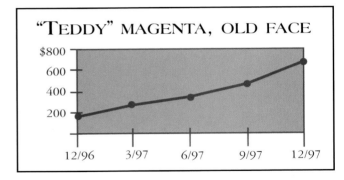

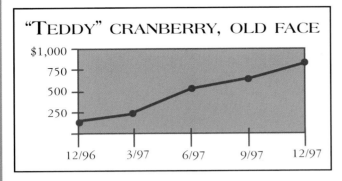

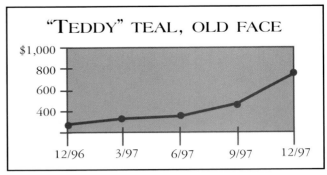

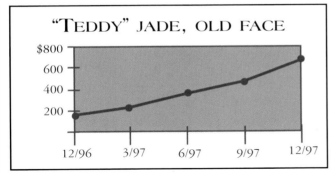

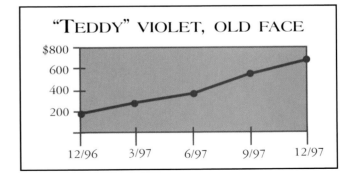

"TRAP" THE MOUSE (R)

Born: N/A
Released: 1994
Retired: 1995
Description: Ty produced quite a cute mouse. His pink ears, feet, and tail give him an unreal-mouse look, which is very good in Trap's case (if he looked like a real mouse, he wouldn't be so lovable). The petite Trap was only in the Beanie Baby fold for about a year and he's about as rare any BB can be. While he wasn't the most popular when he was issued, his value is sky-high today.
Value: $550.00

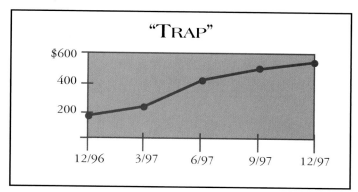

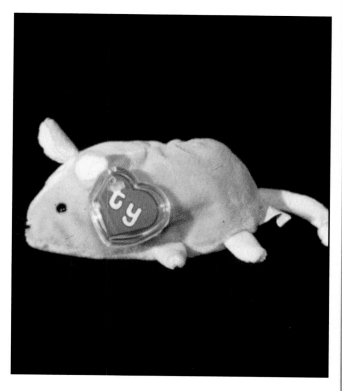

"TUFFY" THE TERRIER

Born: 10 - 12 - 96
Released: May 1997
Description: Tuffy's simple color styling is a big plus, as is his ability to stand on his four legs. He has much more personality than Scottie, a similar-styled Beanie Baby dog. Tuffy's been available in good (but not large) numbers in 1997.
Value: $12.00

"TUSK" THE WALRUS (R)

Born: 9 - 18 - 95
Released: 1996
Retired: January 1997
Error: "Tuck" hang tag
Description: The first Tusks that were sent to stores had the name "Tuck" on the hang tags. Only mildly interesting, this error has not caused too great of a price difference between the error and correct tags. A very nice style, Tusk got an early retirement, probably partially due to the fact that his pal, Jolly, was waiting in the wings. Look for a good future for Tusk.
Value: "Tusk" tag—$65.00; "Tuck" tag—$80.00

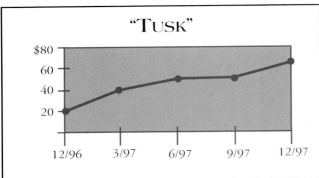

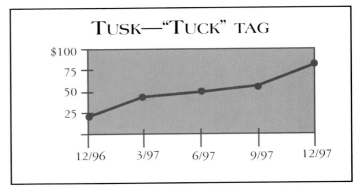

"TWIGS" THE GIRAFFE

Born: 5 - 19 - 95
Released: 1996
Variations: light orange, dark orange (both current)
Description: In many people's opinion, Twigs is the best-designed Beanie Baby ever. He has a sensational style, beautiful colors, and he's a good-sized BB. People who don't like BBs (yes, there are a few of those folks still out there) generally like Twigs. There is a slight difference in the Twigs that were out in 1997. Some were a little lighter orange than the ones that were produced earlier. The difference is noticeable when you put the two varieties next to each other. I've seen both varieties in the same shipments, so it isn't a valuable variation. Twigs was mostly absent in the first half of 1997, and his value rose. But he was out in good numbers over the last half, and his price dropped significantly.
Value: $12.00

"VALENTINO" THE BEAR

Born: 2 - 14 - 94
Released: 1995
Description: A top-10, most popular current Beanie Baby, it seems Valentino has been out forever. This white bear with the red heart over his heart is a perfect St. Valentine's Day gift. Well, Valentino is a great gift anytime. The first white Teddy Bear, Maple and Libearty followed in Valentino's style. Valentino will always remain highly popular. He was out in big numbers for a few months of 1997, but has since taken a sabbatical. Is he going to retire soon? Odds are that he will.
Value: $22.00

"VELVET" THE PANTHER (R)

Born: 12 - 16 - 95
Released: 1995
Retired: Sept. 30, 1997
Description: Velvet is a great panther, and retirement has boosted his popularity. Velvet remains one of the lesser valued retirees. That's due in part to his being available in very large quantities in 1997 (he was spotted in retailer shipments through Nov. 15). It will be some time before Velvet (along with Hoot, Legs, and a few others) begins to see any substantial upward movement in value.
Value: $23.00

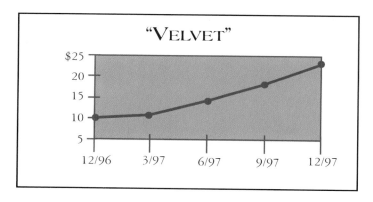

"WADDLE" THE PENGUIN

Born: 12 - 19 - 95
Released: 1995
Description: A big winner in the style department, Waddle is an all-time favorite Beanie Baby. Neatly formed with striking colors, he stands out in a crowd. Waddle was available in decent quantities through 1997.
Value: $10.00

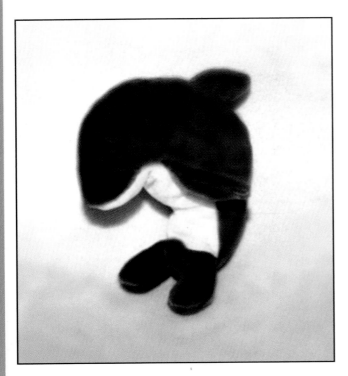

"WAVES" THE WHALE

Born: 12 - 8 - 96
Released: May 1997
Error: Waves with Echo tags
Description: Waves received Echo the dolphin's tags when first issued in 1997. It was really no big deal, as many of these errors were produced. While there is no price difference between the error and correct versions, some Beanie Baby ne'er-do-wells were trying to sell the error versions for big dollars. Waves was out in many waves through 1997.
Value: $12.00

"WEB" THE SPIDER (R)

Born: N/A
Released: 1994
Retired: 1995
Description: With his black coat and eight legs, Web is one of the creepiest Beanie Babies around. Web might have been a seasonal (Halloween) BB, as he was retired rather quickly after his release. A very hard-to-find BB in any condition, Web is high on the list of advanced BB collectors.
Value: $625.00

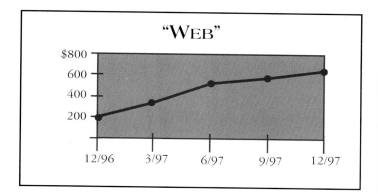

"WEENIE" THE DACHSHUND

Born: 7 - 20 - 95
Released: 1996
Description: Weenie is one of the most realistic-looking Beanie Babies ever made. His expression appears to be one of genuine concern. Concern for what? Who knows? Weenie can be found in two different types of brown cloth: one is a little shinier than the other, but there's no difference in price for either one. Weenie began showing up in big numbers beginning in August 1997, after being absent earlier in the year.
Value: $15.00

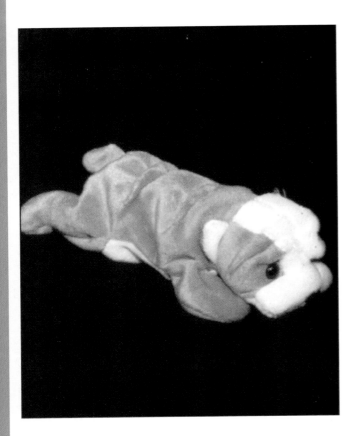

"WRINKLES" THE BULLDOG

Born: 5 - 1 - 96
Released: 1996
Description: The brown and white Wrinkles is an extremely cute Beanie Baby dog. Similar in style to Pugsly, Wrinkles has a forehead full of wrinkles, and he has two wrinkles on his back. A clever style, Wrinkles will always be a popular fellow.
Value: $10.00

"ZIGGY" THE ZEBRA

Born: 12 - 24 - 95
Released: 1995
Variations: thicker and fewer stripes (current), thinner and more stripes (current)
Description: Ziggy is a similar style to Mystic and Derby. However, Ziggy's stripes were eventually changed from thinner and closer together to thicker and farther apart. So far, there is no price difference between the variations.
Value: thicker stripes—$10.00; thinner stripes—$10.00

"ZIP" THE CAT

Born: 3 - 28 - 94

Released: 1995

Variations: black belly with white paws/whiskers/ears (current); all black body with pink ears/pink whiskers (discontinued); white face/belly with pink ears/whiskers (discontinued)

Description: Zip followed the same path as Nip, when it came to variations. The first Zip had a white face and belly, pink ears and whiskers, and the rest of him was black. The second (and rarer version) sported an all-black body, with pink ears and whiskers. The first and second versions were retired in 1995. The current version has white paws, ears and whiskers, and the rest of him is black. The current version was in short supply for most of 1997; by October, however, he was flooding retailer shelves.

Value: black belly/white paws—$13.00; all black—$1,250.00; white belly—$325.00

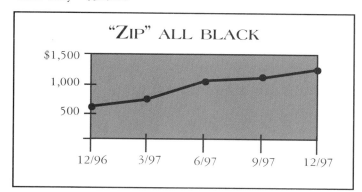

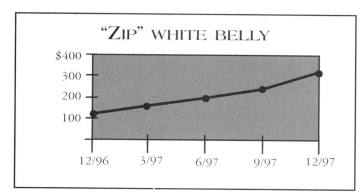

New Beanie Babies

"Britannia" the bear

Born: not available
Released: Dec. 31, 1997
Description: Like the Canada-only Maple, Britannia (with the British flag over his chest) will be a Beanie Baby that will drive U.S. collectors crazy. This BB is reportedly a "Ty Europe Exclusive." What that means, in plain English, is that it will be a very expensive BB to get your hands on. It will probably be a lot tougher than Maple, since many collectors were able to go directly to Canada to get a Maple, or had friends or family in Canada get one for them. From the photo I've seen, Britannia looks like a very beautiful bear.
Value: Not determined at time of writing.

"Bruno" the terrier

Born: 9 - 9 - 97
Released: Dec. 31, 1997
Description: To most collectors' surprise, Ty didn't retire any dogs in the last round of 1997 retirements, but it did add two more pooches to the line (that might mean that several dogs are getting ready for retirement). Bruno is cute—not overly cute—but cute.
Value: Not determined at time of writing.

"Hissy" the snake

Born: 4 - 4 - 97
Released: Dec. 31, 1997
Description: I think Hissy will be one of the more popular of the new releases, based mainly on the fact that almost no one has a Beanie Baby snake in their collection (there aren't many collectors who own Slither).
Value: Not determined at time of writing.

"Iggy" the iguana

Born: 8 - 12 - 97
Released: Dec. 31, 1997
Description: The last new Beanie Babies of 1997 had a decidedly reptilian theme, with a new chameleon, frog, snake, and iguana. Iggy looks pretty cool (almost dinosaur-like). He should be particularly popular as he is the first iguana BB. The first Iggys have "Rainbow" tags.
Value: Not determined at time of writing.

"Pounce" the cat

Born: 8 - 28 - 97
Released: Dec. 31, 1997
Description: Two new cats were released at the end of 1997 (Pounce and Prance), and just one was retired (Nip). Pounce is brown and white, and is quite adorable.
Value: Not determined at time of writing.

"Prance" the cat

Born: 11 - 20 - 97
Released: Dec. 31, 1997
Description: Prance is a gray cat with charcoal stripes, blue eyes, and pink whiskers. There's a good chance a cat or two won't make it through the next round of retirements. Odds are that Zip will be the next to go, since he's been around the longest. However, a surprise retirement of Pounce or Prance isn't out of the question (especially after 1997 Teddy and Snowball were retired after just three months in circulation).
Value: Not determined at time of writing.

"PRINCESS"

Born: N/A

Released: December 1997

Description: Rumors had been swirling for some time that Ty would produce a Beanie Baby for the late Diana, Princess of Wales. Ty announced on Oct. 29, 1997, that it was releasing a BB called "Princess." This purple bear with a rose over her heart was released in December of 1997. Ty is donating all of its profits from Princess to the "Diana, Princess of Wales Memorial Fund." Princess was being pre-sold on Internet auctions from $400 to $600 in the first week of December. Wow! It's unlikely that Princess will ever be a $5 to $10 item. That doesn't mean that you won't be able to find her for $5 or $10, but secondary sellers will likely get from $75 to $150 for quite a long time. No matter what, Princess will fly off the shelves at a rate that will be astounding. Not only will BB collectors all want a Princess or two or three, but hundreds of thousands of people who loved Diana and who are non-Beanie Baby collectors will want one, too. That's why secondary market prices will be so strong.

Value: $275.00

"PUFFER" THE PUFFIN

Born: 11 - 3 - 97

Released: Dec. 31, 1997

Description: This little fellow makes a perfect companion to Waddle. Puffer actually looks like a real puffin (I looked at some puffin pictures and read a bit about puffins on the Internet—see how Beanie Babies can be educational?).

Value: Not determined at time of writing.

"RAINBOW" THE CHAMELEON

Born: 10 - 14 - 97

Released: Dec. 31, 1997

Description: Collectors are excited to get their hands on another tie-dyed Beanie Baby. Rainbow will undoubtedly be a very popular style. Wanna bet that he'll change colors in the future? The first Rainbows have "Iggy" tags.

Value: Not determined at time of writing.

"SMOOCHY" THE FROG

Born: 10 - 1 - 97

Released: Dec. 31, 1997

Description: Goodbye, Legs. . . hello, Smoochy! With his green and yellow coloring, Smoochy appears to have a little more going for him than Legs did.

Value: Not determined at time of writing.

"SPUNKY" THE COCKER SPANIEL

Born: 1 - 14 - 97

Released: Dec. 31, 1997

Description: A really nice color and design will help Spunky become a genuine favorite among collectors. He's a good addition to the BB dog lineup.

Value: Not determined at time of writing.

"STRETCH" THE OSTRICH

Born: 9 - 21 - 97

Released: Dec. 31, 1997

Description: Stretch is perhaps the neatest of the new Beanie Babies. I think Ty does a great job on almost all of its BBs, but I especially like the various birds the company issued in 1997, including Baldy, Doodle/Strut and Gobbles.

Value: Not determined at time of writing.

"Princess"

Photo courtesy of Debby Flynn

SET OF 10 TEENIE BEANIE BABIES

Released: April 1997
Retired: April 1997
Value: $75.00
Description: This is a complete set of 10 mint-in-bag McDonald's Teenie Beanie Babies. Look for this set to rise in value, and especially when, and if, McDonald's has another Teenie Beanie Babies promotion.

SET OF 10 TEENIE BEANIE BABIES

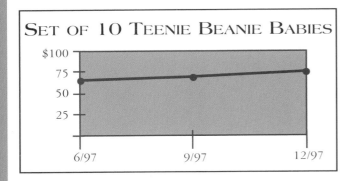

BEANIE BABIES: TEENIE BEANIE BABIES

The McDonald's Teenie Beanie Baby promotion was probably the most important event in Beanie Baby history. This national promotion succeeded in bringing in hundreds of thousands, if not close to a million or more, new Beanie Baby collectors. This promotion made "Beanie Baby" a household word. People who had never heard of Beanie Babies suddenly found themselves standing in line at McDonald's to buy a Happy Meal or five or 10 to get the suddenly hot Teenie Beanie Babies.

The promotion began on April 11, 1997. Immediately, McDonald's restaurants from Sacramento to Kalamazoo felt the crush of collectors eager to get their hands on each of the 10 Teenie Beanie Babies. After the few hours of the promotion on the first day, many McD's had run through the TBBs that were supposed to last them for a week; some were even out of their entire supply in just a few days. It was apparent this five-week promotion wouldn't go the distance; it ended within a couple of weeks. Supposedly, McDonald's had 100 million TBBs made (about 10 million of each style).

The Teenie Beanie Babies themselves are quite well done. About 25% of the size of the original Beanie Babies, the first two in the series (Patti and Pinky) are a little harder to come by than the rest. A complete set (in original packaging) sells for about $75. Out of the package, that price drops to about $20 to $25. In kid-played-with-it-and-chewed-on-it condition . . . no collector value at all, but when kids have fun you can't put a monetary value on that!

"CHOCOLATE" THE MOOSE

#4 of 10
Released: April 1997
Retired: April 1997
Value: $8

"CHOPS" THE LAMB

#3 of 10
Released: April 1997
Retired: April 1997
Value: $10

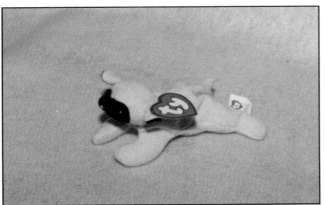

"GOLDIE" THE FISH

#5 of 10
Released: April 1997
Retired: April 1997
Value: $8

"LIZZ" THE LIZARD

#10 of 10
Released: April 1997
Retired: April 1997
Value: $7

"PATTI" THE PLATYPUS

#1 of 10
Released: April 1997
Retired: April 1997
Value: $10

"PINKY" THE FLAMINGO

#2 of 10
Released: April 1997
Retired: April 1997
Value: $14

"QUACKS" THE DUCK

#9 of 10

Released: April 1997
Retired: April 1997
Value: $7

"SEAMORE" THE SEAL

#7 of 10

Released: April 1997
Retired: April 1997
Value: $8

"SNORT" THE BULL

#8 of 10

Released: April 1997
Retired: April 1997
Value: $7

"SPEEDY" THE TURTLE

#6 of 10

Released: April 1997
Retired: April 1997
Value: $8

BEANPALS

Kellytoy, which has been making toys for more than 12 years, has introduced a line of beanies called "Beanpals." Similar to beanbag toys of its competitors, Beanpals are a quality effort and offer collectors a lot of beanies to collect. At the time of this writing, there are 115 "Original" Beanpals, 14 "Hotsy Spotsy" Beanpals, and a limited edition Los Angeles Dodgers Beanpal bear (the bear is dressed in a Dodgers uniform). Beanpals are about 7 1/2 inches long or tall (depending on which way the Beanpal sits). The new "Hotsy Spotsy" Beanpals seem to be particularly popular now. They feature hot colors and spots (thus their name). So far, no Beanpals have been retired. In addition to the regular-size Beanpals, the company has issued a number of smaller versions called "Itsy Bitsy Teeny Weeny Little Mini Beanpal Babies" and "Pocket Beanpals."

Tags: The hang tags (of which there are many styles) include the Beanpals' name.

Availability: Local gift stores, large department stores, gift, and toy store chains. The L.A. Dodgers Beanpals was available at the stadium, but I got mine at the Dodgers Internet site (listed below).

Average retail price: $4.99.

Related Internet sites:
  Beanpals—http://www.beanpals.com/
  L.A. Dodgers—http://www.dodgers.com/

Future collectibility: This line is cute and well-made. They are affordable (you can sometimes find them for less than $5). There is a large variety of characters to collect, whether you're looking to assemble the entire series, or buy a few animals you're fond of. Children, in particular, might enjoy collecting Beanpals. It has been reported to me by a company spokesperson that there are no plans in the near future to retire any Beanpals. If the company does retire some in the future, Beanpals could become more popular on the secondary market, and prices could increase.

"Rosie"

"Hot Spot"

Beanpals Characters

"HOTSY SPOTSY" BEANPALS

Cheddar the mouse—yellow with red spots; current value: $5

Crumpet the frog—light blue with dark blue spots; current value: $5

Holy Cow the cow—yellow with red spots; current value: $5

Hot Diggity the dog—white with blue spots; current value: $5

Hot Dog the dog—yellow with red spots; current value: $5

Hot Frog the frog—yellow with red spots; current value: $5

Hot Spot the dog—light blue with dark blue spots; current value: $5

Hotsy the bunny—yellow with red spots; current value: $5

Pigsby the pig—yellow with red spots; current value: $5

Pigsy the pig—white with red spots; current value: $5

Sharper the dog—white with blue spots; current value: $5

Sharpy the dog—yellow with red spots; current value: $5

Silly Cow the cow—lavender with purple spots; current value: $5

Spotso the hippo—yellow with red spots; current value: $5

"Lambster"

"ORIGINAL" BEANPALS

Alley the cat—white; current value: $5

Andy Pandy the panda bear—black and white; current value: $5

Bass the dog—brown and white; current value: $5

Beau the panther—black; current value: $5

Beavis the bear—brown and tan; current value: $5

Bernie the dog—brown and white; current value: $5

Birdy the bird—blue, yellow, black, and white; current value: $5

Blueberry the frog—blue; current value: $5

Boomer the kangaroo—brown and white; current value: $5

Bronto the dinosaur—green and yellow; current value: $5

Bronty the dinosaur—brown; current value: $5

Bubba the fish—blue and yellow; current value: $5

Bubble the fish—green, red, blue, and yellow; current value: $5

Bubble Gum the bear—white; current value: $5

Bud the bear—white in Santa hat; current value: $5

Buddy the frog—green and yellow; current value: $5

Bumble the bee—yellow; current value: $5

Butch the dog—brown; current value: $5

Butterball the bear—cream; current value: $5

Buttercup the butterfly—yellow and orange; current value: $5

Candy the cat—white; current value: $5

"Nosy"

Casanova the bear—white; current value: $5

Cheerio the cheetah—yellow with brown spots; current value: $5

Cheery the monkey—red and white; current value: $5

Cherry the frog—red; current value: $5

Chester the cheetah—orange with brown spots; current value: $5

Chuck the cow—black and white; current value: $5

Cocoa the reindeer—brown; current value: $5

Corky the dog—brown; current value: $5

Coty the bear—brown; current value: $5

Cracker the parrot—green, yellow, and red; current value: $5

Crewcut the eagle—brown; current value: $5

Crock the crocodile—green; current value: $5

Crocker the crocodile—green; current value: $5

Danny the dog—brown and white; current value: $5

Domino the dalmatian—white with black spots; current value: $5

Doug the dog—white with black spots; current value: $5

Dynamite the bull—red and black; current value: $5

Dyno the dinosaur—green; current value: $5

Ellie the elephant—yellow; current value: $5

Fargo the moose—brown; current value: $5

Feathers the bird—black, white, and tan; current value: $5

Flip the dolphin—grey and white; current value: $5

Freddy the frog—green; current value: $5

Frosty the snowman—white; current value: $5

Garth the dinosaur—tie-dyed; current value: $5

Gerry the giraffe—tan with brown spots; current value: $5

Happy the bird—brown; current value: $5

Hazel the owl—brown and cream; current value: $5

Hip the hippo—pink; current value: $5

Holly the parrot—red, yellow and blue; current value: $5

Hoosier the wolf—grey and white; current value: $5

Juliet the cat—white; current value: $5

Lambster the lamb—green and yellow; current value: $5

Lamby the lamb—pink and white; current value: $5

Larry the lion—tan; current value: $5

Lawrence the dog—white and red; current value: $5

Leggy the spider—white; current value: $5

Leo the lion—tan; current value: $5

"Cherry"

"Cheddar"

"Blueberry"

"Dynamite"

Little Ricky the raccoon—grey, black, and white; current value: $5

Loaner the shark—grey and white; current value: $5

Manfred the manatee—grey; current value: $5

Max the doberman—brown and black; current value: $5

Mega the dinosaur—white and black; current value: $5

Milkdud the cow—black and white; current value: $5

Missy the bear—cream; current value: $5

Moby the whale—black and white; current value: $5

Molly the parrot—green, red, yellow, and blue; current value: $5

Monty the monkey—brown and tan; current value: $5

Mr. Claus—Santa Claus colors; current value: $5

Nosy the elephant—blue and pink; current value: $5

Nuttah the elephant—grey; current value: $5

Patty the bear—white; current value: $5

Paws the bear—tie-dyed; current value: $5

Penny the penguin—black and white; current value: $5

Percy the pig—pink; current value: $5

Philly the horse—brown and white; current value: $5

Polly the parrot—orange and yellow; current value: $5

Polo the bear—white; current value: $5

Purrly the cat—pink and white; current value: $5

Raja the tiger—white with black stripes; current value: $5

Ratty the rat—pink and yellow; current value: $5

Rex the dinosaur—blue; current value: $5

Ricky the raccoon—grey, black and white; current value: $5

Rosie the flamingo—pink and white; current value: $5

Rover the dog—orange and white; current value: $5

Saffron the cat—green; current value: $5

Sammy the seal—white; current value: $5

Samson the bull—brown; current value: $5

Saurus the dinosaur—yellow and black; current value: $5

Scottie the dalmatian—white with black stripes; current value: $5

Sky the bear—blue; current value: $5

Slick the fox—brown and white; current value: $5

Spam the pig—cream; current value: $5

Spot the dog—yellow and brown; current value: $5

Starburst the bird—orange; current value: $5

Stinger the scorpion—brown; current value: $5

Stinker the dinosaur—black and white; current value: $5

Striker the white tiger—white with black stripes; current value: $5

Swanny the swan—white; current value: $5

Tabby the cat—brown, tan and white; current value: $5

Tarrance the spider—black; current value: $5

Tammy the spider—pink; current value: $5

Thermador the lobster—red; current value: $5

Tig the tiger—orange with black stripes; current value: $5

Trippy the bird—tie-dyed; current value: $5

Tony the tiger—orange with black stripes; current value: $5

Trump the elephant—grey; current value: $5

Trunk the elephant—grey; current value: $5

Tuck the turtle—green and white; current value: $5

Tux the penguin—black and white in Santa hat; current value: $5

Tyrone the dinosaur—red and yellow; current value: $5

Wally the walrus—brown; current value: $5

Wings the bear—white; current value: $5

Zig the zebra—white with black stripes; current value: $5

"LIMITED EDITION" BEANPAL

Bearbino, the L.A. Dodgers bear-white bear in Dodgers uniform; current value: $15

"Sharper"

"Alley"

BEAN SPROUTS

When collectors were busy looking for Beanie Babies in the spring and summer of 1997, they often ran across Bean Sprouts. With few Beanie Babies to be had during that time, some collectors began acquiring this line. The original line consisted of a staggering 71 Bean Sprouts. The number of Bean Sprouts produced to date is 102—close to the number of Beanie Babies released by Ty.

Created by Gift Innovations, a division of Great American Fun Corp., the company seems to have changed its strategy in 1997, getting away from traditional colors and releasing more Bean Sprouts in distinct colors, notably tie-dyed and neon. Bean Sprouts has produced 10 tie-dyed and six neon animals to date. These seem to be very popular. The 11 holiday-related Bean Sprouts appear to be successful, as well. The design of some of the early Sprouts was lacking in sophistication, but it looks like the company has improved in that area. There have also been 15 retirements; so far, little interest has been shown on the secondary market.

Tags: The hang tags on the regular Bean Sprouts have the "Bean Sprouts" name and a drawing with four characters on the front side and the name of the Bean Sprout on the back side. They also have tush tags. The holiday-themed Bean Sprouts sport tags that open like a book, with the holiday noted on the front (i.e., "Halloween Bean Sprouts"). Note: Some Bean Sprouts have no names on them; these were sent to retailers for placement in special displays. They are probably worth a few dollars more to a serious collector.

Availability: Bean Sprouts are generally found in gift shops. I've also found them in larger retail stores.

Average retail price: $4

Related Internet site: Bean Sprouts (you can order Bean Sprouts from this site, even many of the retired ones)—
http://www.virtualtoystore.com/sprouts/

Future collectibility: The future collectibility of Bean Sprouts is currently open for debate. It did take Ty several years to reach mass popularity with its Beanie Babies. It is possible that Bean Sprouts could catch on to a larger degree in the next few years. But with all the competition that Bean Sprouts face, it's a tough beanie market out there right now. The company seems to be producing some really nice products, so the quality factor is there, and that's a big plus. Two more factors in this line's favor are price (about $4) and availability (no problem finding most styles). It's likely that the company will continue its color innovations, i.e., tie-dyed and neon. Having some fun with the colors looks like a good way to draw attention and gain a following in the crowded beanie marketplace.

94

Bean Sprouts Characters

retired

Acorn the squirrel—current value: $4

Alex the alligator—current value: $4

Ariel the ostrich—current value: $4

*Bandit the raccoon—retired: Aug. 4, 1997; current value: $5

*Berry the neon bear—retired: Nov. 10, 1997; current value: $6

Billy the blue jay—current value: $4

*Bobo the black bear—retired: Nov. 10, 1997; current value: $6

Boris the spider—see Widow

Bossie the cow—current value: $4

Bruno the tie-dyed brontosaurus—current value: $4

Bubba the tie-dyed T. Rex—current value: $4

Bubble Gum the neon pig—current value: $4

Bucky the beaver—current value: $4

Buford the brown pup—current value: $4

Buttercup the neon cow—current value: $4

Button the snowman—current value: $4

Casanova the Valentine bear—current value: $4

*Claw the crab—retired: Nov. 10, 1997; current value: $5

Cleo the neon cat—current value: $4

Cloppy the horse—current value: $4

Cottontail the bunny—pink; current value: $4

Cottontail the bunny—white; current value: $4

Daisy the tie-dyed cow—see Sunshine

Danny the dalmatian—current value: $4

Dash the dolphin—current value: $4

Domino the orca whale—current value: $4

*Dotty the ladybug—retired: Aug. 4, 1997; current value: $7

Dundee the koala bear—current value: $4

Felix the neon frog—current value: $4

Finster the tropical fish—current value: $4

Freida the goldfish—current value: $4

*Gentle the lamb—retired: Nov. 10, 1997; current value: $5

Godfrey the ghost—current value: $4

Grace the angel—current value: $4

Grand Slam the baseball—current value: $4

Gus the gorilla—current value: $4

Honey the bumblebee—current value: $4

Hornsby the rhino—current value: $4

Howie the wolf—current value: $4

J.R. the terrier—current value: $4

Jumbo the elephant—current value: $4

Kick the soccer ball—current value: $4

Kris Santa—current value: $4

Lana the lobster—current value: $4

Lenny the leopard—current value: $4

Leo the lion—current value: $4

Lilly the tie-dyed frog—current value: $4

Louie the cardinal—current value: $4

Magnolia the tie-dyed horse—current value: $4

Marcel the monkey—current value: $4

Miami the flamingo—current value: $4

Moon the tie-dyed dog—current value: $4

Oasis the camel—current value: $4

Olivia the octopus—current value: $4

Oscar the wiener dog—current value: $4

Owliver the owl—current value: $4

Patches the calico cat—current value: $4

Percy the pelican—current value: $4

Pickles the neon puppy—current value: $4

Ping the penguin—current value: $4

Pockets the kangaroo—current value: $4

Polly the panda—current value: $4

Pounce the tiger—current value: $4

Prince the frog—current value: $4

Princess the poodle—current value: $4

Pudgey the pig—current value: $4

Rags the scarecrow—current value: $4

Rocky the rooster—current value: $4

Romeo the Valentine bear—current value: $4

Roland the reindeer—current value: $4

*Roosevelt the bear—retired: Nov. 10, 1997; current value: $6

Rosie the tie-dye pig—current value: $4

Sally the seal—current value: $4

*Salty the sea lion—retired: Aug. 4, 1997; current value: $5

*Sammy the skunk—retired: Nov. 10, 1997; current value: $5

Sasha the polar bear—current value: $4

Slam the basketball—current value: $4

Sly the fox—current value: $4

Snaps the dragon—current value: $4

*Spumoni the tie-dye bear—retired: Nov. 10, 1997; current value: $6

Squeaky the mouse—current value: $4

Stanley the tie-dye triceratops—current value: $4

Stretch the giraffe—current value: $4

Stewy the tie-dye stegosaurus—current value: $4

Sunshine the tie-dye cow—with Daisy hang tag; current value: $4

Sweets the gingerbread man—current value: $4

*Sydney the snake—retired: Aug. 4, 1997; current value: $5

Tabby the cat—current value: $4

*Tee the manatee—retired: Aug. 4, 1997; current value: $5

*Tiki the toucan—retired: Aug. 4, 1997; current value: $5

Tommy the turtle—current value: $4

Torro the bull—current value: $4

Touchdown the football—current value: $4

*Twinkle the starfish—retired: Aug. 4, 1997; current value: $5

Vinnie the vulture—current value: $4

*Wally the walrus—retired: Aug. 4, 1997; current value: $5

Webster the duck—current value: $4

Whitey the shark—current value: $4

Widow the spider—with Boris hang tag; current value: $4

Wing the Pegasus—current value: $4

Winston the bulldog—current value: $4

Yakky the parrot—current value: $4

Zak the zebra—current value: $4

Zelda the witch—current value: $4

CHEF JR. BEANBAG BUDDIES

There were several beanie toy offers in 1997 that required the purchase of a food product. The Chef Jr. Beanbag Buddies set was among them. For each of the Beanbag Buddies, you were required to send the proofs of purchase from four cans of Chef Jr. Boyardee products, along with an original order form and $1.25 for postage/handling. Each toy was sent separately, even if you ordered the whole set; thus, the high amount of postage for all six—$7.50. Add in the cost of the 24 cans of food, and it made for a pretty expensive set of beanies. However, if you are a Chef Jr. Boyardee fan, as I am (yum-yum), the set essentially cost $7.50, which is pretty reasonable.

Tags: Beanbag Buddies have no hang tags, but do have tush tags that give the name of each character.

Availability: The offer ends on July 31, 1998. After that date, you'll have to find this set on the secondary market.

Average retail price: $4

Future collectibility: Primitive in appearance, Beanbag Buddies are nonetheless cute, mostly because they're smaller than the average beanie toy (none longer than 7 inches, and none taller than 6 inches). Because collectors had to buy many cans of food to get this set, these advertising premiums are likely not all that common. The two dinosaurs and the dog are the best of the bunch. It isn't known if this will be the one-and-only set of these to appear, or if there will be more in the future. A future set would add to the collectibility of the first set.

Chef Jr. Beanbag Buddies Characters

Christy the sea horse—current value: $4

Jumbo the whale—current value: $4

Rex the tyrannosaurus rex—current value: $4

Rigatoni the dog—current value: $4

Sharkeel the shark—current value: $4

Steggy the stegosaurus—current value: $4

CLIFFORD THE BIG RED DOG

One of the finer efforts of 1997 was the beanbag toy featuring Clifford the Big Red Dog of children's stories written by Norman Bridwell. Good material, good color, and a good likeness make Clifford one of the best beanies of the year. Measuring 7 inches from nose to foot, Clifford was issued by Scholastic.

Tags: The hang tag is blue and yellow, and has Clifford on the front, with information about Clifford on the inside. He has a big tush tag.

Availability: Not the easiest beanie to track down, I found mine at a book/record store at an area mall. You might have to do some hunting for this fellow.

Average retail price: $6.50

Related Internet site: Scholastic—http://scholastic.com/

Future collectibility: Clifford seems to have been produced in small numbers. He's a popular character, and this beanie might be on collectors' want-lists in the future. By the way, the first Clifford book was published in 1963.

Current value: $10

COCA-COLA BEAN BAG PLUSH

When Dr. John Pemberton invented Coca-Cola in the late 1800s, he couldn't have been thinking, "And someday they'll make Coca-Cola beanies." But that's just what happened! Coca-Cola has issued two sets of six beanbag toy collectibles based on its characters (polar bear, penguin, and seal). A third set was released in January 1998, titled the "Coca-Cola Heritage Collection" (at the time of this writing, I had only seen a drawing of these beanies). Other sets will likely be out in 1998, as well. Beautifully executed, these beanies are a top-flight effort. Visually appealing, they are extra nice for collectors as the sets are small and currently reasonably priced. Both of the first two sets were reportedly retired. These beanies were made by Cavanaugh, the same company that made the Harley-Davidson Bean Bag Plush.

Tags: The Coca-Cola beanies' tags are bottle cap-shaped. The tags are silver, and the name of the beanie is on the inside of the tags. Each beanie also has a tush tag.

Availability: The first two sets of beanies were available at stores such as Target and Walgreen's. I also saw the first two sets at my local grocery store in December of 1997, for $4.99 per beanie. Dealers who carry limited edition Coca-Cola items and other beanie products also have these in stock.

Average retail price: The first 12 beanies were available for regular retail of $5 to $6 each at the end of 1997. However, prices from some dealers were as high as $15 each. Many were priced at $8 apiece.

Related Internet site: Coca-Cola—http://www.cocacola.com/

Future collectibility: A high rating for the future of these frosty beanies. Like other character beanies, more than one group will be collecting them. Both Coca-Cola and beanie collectors will be vying for these beanies. Add the fact that the first two sets were retired not long after they were released, and you can see there is the possibility for an increase in value over the coming years.

"1st Series"

100

Coca-Cola Bean Bag Plush Characters

*retired

*1st Series, "Spring 1997,"
issued spring 1997

Penguin with delivery hat—current value: $8
Polar Bear with Coca-Cola baseball hat—current value: $8
Polar Bear—current value: $8
Polar Bear with Coca-Cola shirt—current value: $8
Polar Bear with red bow—current value: $8
Seal with baseball hat—current value: $8

*2nd Series, "Holiday,"
issued in fall 1997

Penguin with Coca-Cola stocking hat—current value: $8
Polar Bear with Coca-Cola stocking hat—current value: $8
Polar Bear with plaid bow tie—current value: $8
Polar Bear with red bow—current value: $8
Seal with red and white scarf—current value: $8
Seal with red and white stocking hat—current value: $8

3rd Series, "Heritage,"
issued January 1998

(These descriptions are based on a drawing; the actual beanies might be different.)
Coca-Cola can with hat—current value: $7
Polar Bear with hat and shirt—current value: $7
Polar Bear with hat and bow tie—current value: $7
Moose—current value: $7
Seal with hat—current value: $7
Walrus—current value: $7

"2nd Series"

DISNEY MINI BEAN BAGS

Take the hottest toy around (beanies) and blend in the most popular characters in the world (Disney) and you can readily see why Disney Mini Bean Bags are as popular as they are. At the time of this writing, there were more than 50 different characters available, with some having several variations. These variation beanies were initially selling for about $10, but they began increasing in value toward the end of 1997. The first 11 Disney Mini Bean Bags (test issues) debuted in select Disney Stores and at Disney Theme Parks in 1997. Many of these test beanies were different from the regular versions which hit stores and parks later in the year. Disney has steadily added to this popular line, and it doesn't appear to be losing steam. Expect many more Disney Mini Bean Bags in 1998 and beyond. Watch for style changes and short-run beanies, such as the holiday Disney Mini Bean Bags, and Flubber.

Tags: Tags include the Disney Store tags, Mouseketoy tags (available at theme parks), Club Disney tags (available at Club Disney) and Classic Pooh tags. Sometimes, the tags have incorrect measurements (i.e., saying the beanie is 7 inches when it's really 8 inches). Where measurements are listed in the price guide, they are the actual measurements of the beanies, not what's on the tags.

Availability: Through the Disney Store and at Disney Theme Parks, as well as through many secondary market sellers. Some are available by pre-purchasing videos at the Disney Store.

Average retail price: $6 at the Disney Store and at Disney Theme Parks.

Related Internet site: The Disney Store Online— http://store.disney.com/

Future collectibility: I think that of all the beanies listed in this book, Disney Mini Bean Bags have the second-best future collectibility, behind Ty's Beanie Babies. Beanie collectors seem to be just beginning to buy Disney Mini Bean Bags on a regular basis. I expect more beanie fans to gravitate toward these Disney-character beanies in 1998. Add to that mix the number of dedicated Disney collectors (there are tens of thousands of serious Disney collectors), and you can begin to see the potential for the Disney Mini Bean Bags. Expect the early test versions to continue to escalate in price as hobbyists go back to complete their collections.

Disney Mini Bean Bags Characters

*retired

"101 DALMATIANS"

101 Dalmatians pup—Style 1; test issue; blue collar; no spots on belly; "V" on face; padded feet; current value: $40

101 Dalmatians pup—Style 2; blue collar; spots on belly; no "V" on face; seamed feet; current value: $25

101 Dalmatians pup—Style 3; blue collar; spots on belly; "V" on face; seamed feet; current value: $10

*Jewel—pink collar; retired December 1997; current value: $15

Lucky—blue collar; current value: $10

"ALADDIN"

Abu—current value: $10

Genie—current value: $10

"ARISTOCATS"

Marie—current value: $10

"BAMBI"

Bambi—current value: $10

Flower—current value: $10

Thumper—current value: $10

"FLUBBER"

*Flubber—retired December 1997; current value: $12

"HERCULES"

**Pain—current value: $12+

**Panic—current value: $12+

*Pegasus—retired December 1997; current value: $15

**available by pre-ordering "Hercules" video before Feb. 2, 1998

"LADY AND THE TRAMP"

Lady—current value: $10

Tramp—current value: $10

"LION KING"

Nala—current value: $10

Pumbaa—current value: $10

Simba—current value: $10

Timon—current value: $10

"LITTLE MERMAID FRIENDS"

*Flounder—Style 1; test issue; larger than regular version; retired December 1997; current value: $18

*Flounder—Style 2; smaller than test issue; retired December 1997; current value: $12

*Sebastian—Style 1; test issue: seam on back; retired December 1997; current value: $20

*Sebastian—Style 2; no seam on back; retired December 1997; current value: $12

"MICKEY & FRIENDS"

Daisy—current value: $10

Donald—current value: $10

Dumbo—current value: $10

Goofy—Style 1; test issue; larger hat; tag "Mini Bean Bag Goofy;" 9 inches; current value: $25

Goofy—Style 2; smaller hat; tag "Mini Bean Bag Goofy;" current value: $10

Mickey—Style 1; test issue; 9 inches; no black stitching around eyes; current value: $45

Mickey—Style 2; 8 inches; black stitching around eyes; current value: $20

Mickey—Style 3; 7 inches; black stitching around eyes; current value: $10

*Mickey (Santa)—8 inches; retired December 1997; current value: $18

Mickey (Valentine's)—current value: $12

Minnie—Style 1; test issue; 9 inches; no black stitching around eyes; current value: $45

Minnie—Style 2; 8 inches; black stitching around eyes; current value: $20

Minnie—Style 3; 7 inches; black stitching around eyes; current value: $10

*Minnie (Santa)—8 inches; retired December 1997; current value: $18

Minnie (Valentine's)—current value: $12

Pluto—Style 1; test issue; longer tail and ears; tag "Mini Bean Bag Pluto;" 9 inches; current value: $20

Pluto—Style 2; shorter tail and ears; tag "Mini Bean Bag Pluto;" current value: $10

Pluto (Reindeer)—Mouseketoy tags; current value: $25

"PINNOCHIO"

Figaro—current value: $10

Geppetto—current value: $10

Jiminy Crickett—current value: $10

Pinnochio–current value: $10

"POOH & FRIENDS"

Eeyore—Style 1; test issue; tush tag sewn in left leg; current value: $15

Eeyore—Style 2; tush tag sewn under tail; current value: $10

Eeyore (Classic)— "Classic" tags; current value: $10

*Eeyore (Reindeer)—current value: $15

Piglet—Style 1; test issue; foot pads; current value: $35

Piglet—Style 2; no foot pads; current value: $10

Piglet (Classic)—"Classic" tags; current value: $10

Tigger—Style 1; test issue; straight tail; foot pads; thin stripes; current value: $45

Tigger—Style 2; curled tail; no foot pads; thin stripes; current value: $20

Tigger—Style 3; curled tail; no foot pads; thick stripes; brighter orange; current value: $10

Tigger (Classic)—"Classic" tags; current value: $10

Tigger (Santa)—Mouseketoy tags; current value: $25

Winnie the Pooh—Style 1; test issue; foot pads; hard felt nose; current value: $35

Winnie the Pooh—Style 2; no foot pads; stitched nose; current value: $20

Winnie the Pooh—Style 3; no foot pads; hard felt nose; current value: $10

Winnie the Pooh (Classic)—"Classic" tags; current value: $10

*Winnie the Pooh (Santa)—Style 1; hard felt nose; retired December 1997; current value: $22

*Winnie the Pooh (Santa)—Style 2; stitched nose; retired December 1997; current value: $18

Winnie the Pooh (Santa with scarf)—Mouseketoy tags; current value: $25

Winnie the Pooh (Valentine's)—current value: $12

"SEVEN DWARFS"

Bashful—current value: $10

Doc—current value: $10

Dopey—Style 1; tag reads, "Beanbag;" current value: $12

Dopey—Style 2; tag reads, "Bean Bag;" current value: $10

Grumpy—Style 1; tag reads, "Beanbag;" current value: $25

Grumpy—Style 2; tag reads, "Bean Bag;" current value: $10

Happy—current value: $10

Sleepy—current value: $10

Sneezy—current value: $10

"TOY STORY"

Alien—current value: $10

Buzz Lightyear—current value: $10

Woody—current value: $10

Energizer Bunny Bean Bag Toy

He keeps going and going—then he becomes a beanie! Love him or hate him, the Energizer Bunny is available in beanie form. He measures in at 7 inches tall, and he's wearing sunglasses and beating his little Energizer drum with red and white drumsticks. The bunny has a black plastic nose, and contains beans only in his belly—the rest of him is plush. My Energizer Bunny beanie appears different than the Bunny beanie depicted on the order form, although I haven't heard if the order-form version of the beanie character was ever issued.

Tags: A pair of tush tags.

Availability: You could get the bunny through a special mail-in offer, for $2.99 plus two proofs of purchase from any Energizer battery packs. The offer ended March 31, 1998, or while supplies lasted. There was a limit of 10 per household.

Average retail price: $10.

Future collectibility: It appears that Energizer will continue to use the Energizer Bunny as its spokes-character for years to come. The renowned Bunny has become something of an icon in contemporary American culture. This beanie is a well-made item and should remain popular for the foreseeable future. As a side note: Oddly enough, the strap attached to the bunny's drum is connected by Velcro in the back, but the drum itself is permanently sewn into his belly; so the straps can be undone, but the drum stays in place.

Energizer Bunny Bean Bag Toy

Energizer Bunny—current value: $10

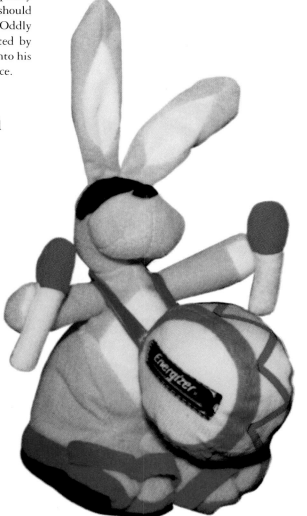

GENERAL MILLS BIG G BREAKFAST BABIES

General Mills probably cashed-in big-time with its yummy set of seven Big G Breakfast Babies, which featured the company's most popular cereal characters. Nicely executed, these beanies follow the look of the characters to a "T," from their colors to their costumes. One of my favorite sets (and some of my favorite cereals), I was glad to see General Mills had the foresight to issue such a set.

Tags: The hang tags are light blue with a picture of each character's cereal. The inside has a story and the name of the Big G Breakfast Baby.

Availability: The first cereal boxes announcing the availability of this set were in stores in August or September 1997. Customers had to send special UPCs from two boxes of cereal for each Big G Breakfast Baby, and 50 cents for shipping. At $2.50 a box for 14 boxes of cereal, and $3.50 for shipping, the complete set of seven cost almost $40. But, like other food-beanie offers, if you ate the cereal, the set cost just $3.50. A very good deal! If you didn't want to buy the cereal, you could purchase the Big G Breakfast Babies for $4.99 each, plus shipping (about $40 total). The cereals involved in this promotion were: Trix, Lucky Charms, Kix, Honey Nut Cheerios, Cinnamon Toast Crunch, French Toast Crunch, Count Chocula, Cookie Crisp, and Cocoa Puffs. The offer ends on May 31, 1998, or while supplies last.

Average retail price: $6.

Future collectibility: With the number of cereal premium and beanie collectors, this set should prove to be a highly popular one for a long time. The most popular characters will probably be the Trix Rabbit, Lucky, Sonny the Cuckoo Bird, and Count Chocula.

General Mills Big G Breakfast Babies Characters

Chip the Cookie Hound—character from Cookie Crisp cereal; current value: $6

Count Chocula—character from Count Chocula cereal; current value: $6

Honey Nut Cheerios Bee—character from Honey Nut Cheerios cereal; current value: $6

Lucky the Leprechaun—character from Lucky Charms cereal; current value: $6

Sonny the Cuckoo Bird—character from Cocoa Puffs cereal; current value: $6

Trix Rabbit—character from Trix cereal; current value: $6

Wendell the Baker—character from French Toast Crunch cereal; current value: $6

GRATEFUL DEAD BEANIE BEARS

Grateful Dead Beanie Bears get my vote as the most unusual and inventive of the year. Based on characters from songs of the legendary musical group, the Grateful Dead, the set currently consists of 11 beanies, all about 7 1/2 inches high. Their style and colors are fantastic. These beanies are produced by Liquid Blue, a company that makes other licensed Grateful Dead collectibles (along with licensed items for Paul McCartney, Jimi Hendrix, and Pink Floyd, among other big names). A Liquid Blue spokesman I talked with said that there were plans for more Grateful Dead Beanie Bears in the future.

Tags: In keeping with the unusual, Grateful Dead Beanie Bears don't have hang tags, but do have credentials around their necks. The laminated, full-color tags contain the bear's name, birth date (which corresponds to an epic show date and venue), as well as a "Favorite Tour Memory" from the Grateful Dead (fact or fiction). For example, Cosmic Charlie's favorite memory is: "My white '68 bus broke down on the way to Chicago when a police car pulled up. I thought I was going to get hassled for sure, but instead the cop was a Deadhead and had a bus himself! He helped me fix it and we've traded tapes ever since."

Availability: At the time of writing, many styles were sold out and these beanies were not easy to get. You'll have to locate a retailer who sells them, as they are a little out of the norm for many retailers.

Average retail price: $8

Related Internet site: Liquid Blue—http://www.liquidblue.com/

Future collectibility: Three groups of people will have an interest in collecting Grateful Dead Beanie Bears: 1) Grateful Dead fans; 2) beanie fans; and 3) bear collectors. In baseball, that's a triple play! For these beanies, that means a good future. With more Beanie Bears on the way, it's likely interest will remain strong in this set. I've heard no word on when or if retirements will be happening, but this is the beanie world, and a lot of companies are retiring their beanies.

Grateful Dead Beanie Bears Characters

Althea—birthday, 8/12/79; birthplace, Red Rocks; current value: $12

Bertha—birthday, 5/30/71; birthplace, Winterland; current value: $12

Cassidy—birthday, 9/14/90; birthplace, MSG; current value: $12

Cosmic Charlie—birthday, 1/8/66; birthplace, the Fillmore; current value: $12

Delilah—birthday, 6/21/80; birthplace, West High Auditorium; current value: $12

Jack Straw—birthday, 7/4/86; birthplace, Rich Stadium; current value: $12

St. Stephen—birthday, 9/20/70; birthplace, Fillmore East; current value: $12

Samson—birthday, 6/21/80; birthplace, West High Auditorium; current value: $12

Stagger Lee—birthday, 5/10/97; birthplace, Winterland; current value: $12

Sugaree—birthday, 4/12/82; birthplace, Nassau Coliseum; current value: $12

Tennessee Jed—birthday: 6/27/87; birthplace: Alpine Valley; current value: $12

GUND

Gund beanies are a personal favorite of mine. The company, which has been producing plush toys for many years, and has a great reputation for quality, has several really neat lines of beanies. Although the beanies are priced above other beanie lines, there's a good reason for it—the beanies are very high quality. As far as I know, these are all 1997 releases.

Here is a rundown of the various lines offered:

BABAR BEANIES: A two-beanie set from the children's books based on the character of Babar. Babar is joined by Celeste. I've seen Babar a lot, but not Celeste. They retail for $12 each.

BABE BEANIES: From the movie "Babe," Gund produced a four-beanie set. I've only seen photos of these so far, but they look great. They retail for $8 each.

BARNEY BEANIES: From the popular children's television show featuring Barney the dinosaur comes a two-beanie set (Barney and Baby Bop). Neither has been very easy to locate. Small children especially love these (and parents are glad to buy them for them). They retail for $8 each.

CLASSIC POOH BEANIES: Winnie the Pooh and friends come to life in this set of "Classic Pooh" beanies. These are truly cool Pooh beanies. The Classic Pooh beanies retail for $12 each, and are available in most areas in small but good numbers. Piglet comes in two different colors: a grayish-green body and a soft-green body. It appears the grayish-green version might have been the first release; however, I have no confirmation of this.

CURIOUS GEORGE BEANIE: This is just Curious George at this time (no sign of the man with the yellow hat). A tall beanie that measures some 10 1/2 inches high, he's a little light on the beans (just a smattering of beans in his behind). This children's story favorite has been widely available at $12 retail.

DILBERT BEANIES: This is a five-beanie set from Scott Adams' wildly successful (and funny) comic strip. These have been in good supply. They retail for $10 each.

GUND MALT-O-MEAL BEANIES: Gund and Malt-O-Meal teamed-up to offer three Gund beanies. The box showed that you would get Dahling, Mooky, and Flash with a light green belly (I got the first two and an all-green Flash). For each of these beanies, you had to buy two boxes (six total) of Malt-O-Meal, and add $3 ($9 total). In essence, each beanie cost about $8, but if you ate the Malt-O-Meal, it was really just $3 each. These three beanies, while premiums for buying Malt-O-Meal, do not have any Malt-O-Meal advertising on them. They are actually the same ones you can buy from retailers in the Gund beanie animal set. This offer ends Dec. 31, 1999, or while supplies last.

GUND ANIMAL BEANIES: This set does not have an official name that I know of, so I've just dubbed it the "Gund beanie animal set." In addition to the three beanies from the Malt-O-Meal offer, there are nine others, for a total of 12. So far, these beanies (except for all-green Flash, and Flash with a yellow belly) have not been easy to find. They retail for $7 each.

Tags: The hang tags vary, depending on the line. Each beanie has a hang tag and tush tag.

Availability: Mostly in gift shops and book stores.

Internet resources: http://www.gund.com

Future collectibility: Even though the cost for Gund beanies is higher than other beanies, it appears there aren't nearly as many being produced as other lines. With high quality and smaller numbers made (along with the fact that most lines have a tie-in with a character), Gund beanies should be highly collectible for years to come.

Gund Characters

"ANIMAL BEANIES"

Dahling the ostrich—brown; current value: $7

Flash the frog—all green; current value: $7

Flash the frog—green with yellow belly; current value: $7

Flash the frog—green with light green belly; current value: $7

Mooky the walrus—pink; current value: $7

Puddles the dog—light brown; current value: $7

Rainbow Racer the turtle—multicolored; current value: $7

Slider the floppy bear—current value: $7

Snuffy the sitting bear—chocolate brown; current value: $7

Snuffy the sitting bear—tan brown; current value: $7

Tender Teddy the bear—dark brown; current value: $7

Tinkle the inch worm—multicolored; current value: $7

"BABAR"

Babar the elephant—current value: $12

Celeste the elephant—current value: $12

"BABE"

Babe the pig—current value: $8

Ferdinand the goose—current value: $8

Fly the dog—current value: $8

Maa the sheep—current value: $8

"BARNEY"

Baby Bop the green dinosaur—current value: $8
Barney the purple dinosaur—current value: $8

"CLASSIC POOH"

Pooh the bear—current value: $12
Eeyore the donkey—current value: $12
Kanga the kangaroo—current value: $12
Tigger the tiger—current value: $12
Piglet the Pig—grayish-green; current value: $12
Piglet the Pig—soft green; current value: $12

"CURIOUS GEORGE"

Curious George the monkey—current value: $12

"DILBERT"

Boss—current value: $10

Catbert the cat—current value: $10

Dilbert—current value: $10

Dogbert the dog—current value: $10

Ratbert the rat—current value: $10

HALLMARK'S BABY NIKKI

Hallmark, a $3 billion-plus corporation that's been in business since 1910, is the largest greeting cards organization in the world. Additionally, it creates thousands of gifts, ornaments, paper goods and collectibles. This year, Hallmark released an adorable bean-bag plush dog named "Baby Nikki" (there are also larger plush versions of Nikki). This cute dog is brown and white with a red collar. When I went to the store to get it, I was pleasantly surprised by its cute little face sticking out at me from the shelf. This pooch gets a high rating from me.

Tags: The hang tag is square and red with Baby Nikki's name, Hallmark logo and price.

Availability: Hallmark stores.

Average retail price: $4.95

Related Internet site: Hallmark—http://www.hallmark.com/

Future collectibility: Hallmark collectibles are generally very well made, and this pup fits into that category. Although it appears to be available in ample quantities, if Nikki is retired right after the holiday season, its value might increase. I hope that Hallmark issues a new holiday beanie annually.

Hallmark's Baby Nikki

Baby Nikki—released: December 1997; current value: $5

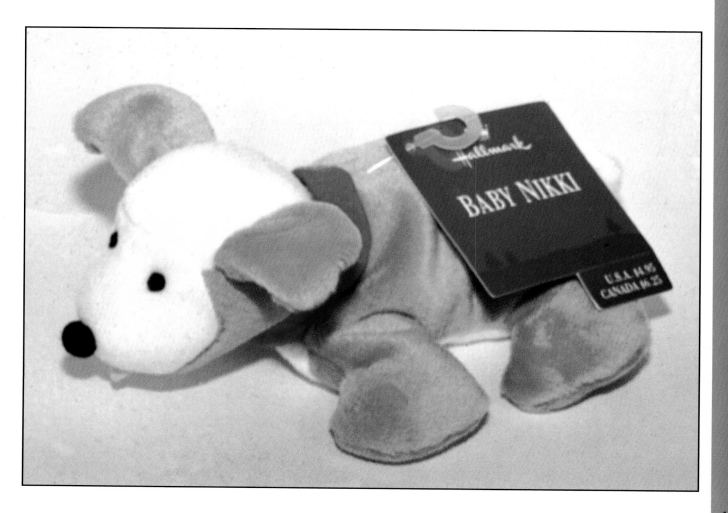

HARLEY-DAVIDSON BEAN BAG PLUSH

The Harley-Davidson Motor Company, makers of the world's most famous motorcycles, began business in 1903. Over the past few years, this Milwaukee-based company has started to heavily market toys and collectibles, finding that there are plenty of willing buyers of Harley-related products. Even those who don't own a Harley motorcycle collect Harley memorabilia. One of the latest creations is a set of six Harley-Davidson Bean Bag Plush characters—three pigs and three bears. Like all Harley products, this set of 6-inch high beanies is first rate, with plenty of beans, good material and nice accouterments. For instance, one bear has a riding hat and boots, and one pig has a head-band and a jean jacket with a zipper that works. There's plenty of nice detail in this set produced by Cavanaugh, the same company that makes the Coca-Cola Bean Bag Plush. For the company's 95th anniversary, plans are in the works for a second series of Harley beanies, which is supposed to include a bull dog.

Tags: The hang tags are square, and contain the company's logo, name of the beanie, and a poem. Each beanie has a tush tag, also.

Availability: The set, which became widely available in late November 1997, can be purchased from a variety of beanie retailers, as well as dealers who carry Harley-Davidson items.

Average retail price: $8

Related Internet site: Harley-Davidson Motor Company— http://www.harley-davidson.com/

Future collectibility: A quality effort and a hot name (Harley) might spell a good future for these beanies. Other limited-edition Harley items have fared well on the secondary market.

Harley-Davidson Bean Bag Plush Characters

Big Twin bear—riding hat and black boots; current value: $8

Motorhead bear—black vest with white trim; current value: $8

Punky pig—jean vest and orange bandanna; current value: $8

Racer pig—red T-shirt and gray bandanna; current value: $8

Rachet pig—black vest; current value: $8

Roamer bear—black T-shirt and red bandanna; current value: $8

KELLOGG'S BEAN BAG BREAKFAST BUNCH

"Snap, Crackle, Pop . . . Rice Krispies!" Kellogg's introduced its own line of beanies called the "Bean Bag Breakfast Bunch." The Rice Krispies trio of Snap!, Crackle!, and Pop! were available by filling out an official order form which appeared on specially marked boxes of Kellogg's Razzle Dazzle Rice Krispies. The completed form, submitted with $8.99, brought a set three characters (the offer ends Dec. 31, 1998, or while supplies last). The trio measures about 7 1/2 inches tall, and they are rather crudely made when compared to the other characters in this assortment. The other Kellogg's characters are Tony the Tiger, Toucan Sam, Dig 'Em the frog, and Cornelius (Corny) the rooster. These animal figures are light years ahead of the Rice Krispies trio in quality (much larger and made of better material). I found these four beanies at my local grocery store, offered as premiums for buying Kellogg's cereal (one beanie per three boxes of cereal). Another store had them for sale at $6.99 each. Additionally, if you ordered the Rice Krispies trio, you received an order form to get Tony the Tiger and Toucan Sam (but not Dig 'Em and Corny, strangely enough).

Tags: The hang tags are like a trading card, and contain a picture of the character on the front and the character's name, year born, favorite cereal, and a "Character"istic on the back (for example, Tony the Tiger's "Character"istic is, "Gr-r-reat!").

Availability: Through special mail-in offers and store giveaways, as well as secondary market sellers.

Average retail price: $7

Related Internet site: Kellogg's—http://kelloggs.com/

Future collectibility: This set should be pretty popular, as there are both beanie collectors and cereal premium collectors who will want them. The toughest-to-get beanies from this set will probably be Dig 'Em and Corny, since they weren't available in the mail-in offer.

Kellogg's Bean Bag Breakfast Bunch Characters

Cornelius—character from Kellogg's Corn Flakes; birth year, 1958; current value: $7

Crackle!—character from Kellogg's Rice Krispies; birth year, 1933; current value: $7

Dig 'Em—character from Kellogg's Smacks; birth year, 1972; current value: $7

Pop!—character from Kellogg's Rice Krispies; birth year, 1933; current value: $7

Snap!—character from Kellogg's Rice Krispies; birth year, 1933; current value: $7

Tony the Tiger—character from Kellogg's Frosted Flakes; birth year, 1952; current value: $7

Toucan Sam—character from Kellogg's Froot Loops; birth year, 1963; current value: $7

McDonald's Floppy Dolls

Three classic characters of the fast-food giant McDonald's have been made into beanie toys—Ronald McDonald, Grimace, and Hamburglar. It's a nice little set of beanies of medium quality. The nice touches include the Hamburglar's hat and cape, and Ronald's cool, red string hair.

Tags: No hang tags, but these beanies do have sewn-in foot tags.

Availability: I ordered my set at the McDonald's Internet site through Group II Communications (800-358-3869) for $15, plus $3 shipping.

Average retail price: $5

Related Internet site: McDonald's—http://www.mcdonalds.com/

Future collectibility: While not of the same quality as some other beanies, this McDonald's trio is a nice addition to your collection, especially if you collect McDonald's toys. If not produced in big quantities, they could scoot-up in price in the coming years, due to the large number of McDonald's collectors.

McDonald's Floppy Dolls Characters

Grimace—7 inches high; current value: $5

Hamburglar—7 inches high; current value: $5

Ronald McDonald—8 inches high; current value: $5

Meanies

Irreverent, repulsive, gross—three words often used to describe Meanies. Meanies are strange and different beanies—a spoof of every cute beanbag toy that's ever been produced. One of the character's names is "Hurley the Pukin' Toucan." That should give you a good idea as to what these particular beanies are all about. Spoofing cute and cuddly things isn't new. Do you remember the Garbage Pail Kids cards that lampooned Cabbage Patch dolls? That's sort of what Meanies are doing to beanies. Well-constructed, Meanies seem to be catching on among collectors and beanie-dislikers alike. Produced by TOPKAT, LLC, the first set of 12 Meanies was introduced October 1, 1997. A Mystery Meanie was added in mid-December. Collectors could obtain the Mystery Meanie by purchasing all 12 original Meanies and sending the 12 proofs of purchase, along with $2.95, to the manufacturer by December 31, 1998. A second set of Meanies was planned.

Tags: These creatures have large, colorful hang tags that have the Meanies' names and a humorous limerick.

Availability: Through gift shops and major retail stores.

Average retail price: $5

Related Internet site: Meanies—http://meanies.com/

Future collectibility: At present, Meanies are a popular novelty. It is possible that they could catch on as a legitimate collectible. Keep in mind that the Garbage Pail Kids cards endured through more than 10 different series, and that cards from the first few series still command a premium price.

Meanies Characters

"1st Series," released Oct. 1, 1997

Armydillo Dan—current value: $6

Bart the Elephart—current value: $6

Boris the Mucousaurus—current value: $6

Fi & Do the Dalmutation—current value: $6

Hurley the Pukin' Toucan—current value: $6

Matt the Fat Bat—current value: $6

Mystery Meanie—current value: $10+

Navy Seal—current value: $6

Otis the Octapunk—current value: $6

Peter the Gotta Peegull—current value: $6

Sledge the Hammered Head Shark—current value: $6

Snake Eyes Jake—current value: $6

Splat the Road Kill Kat—current value: $6

NBC BEANY PEACOCK

This is one of the more unique and highly sought beanies of 1997. The famous NBC Peacock beanie is sold only through NBC for a rather hefty $10, plus $5 for shipping. If you don't mind spending $15, it's a very nicely executed and colorful 6 inch high beanie.

Tags: Only a tush tag that identifies the maker as "Steven Smith."

Availability: Only through NBC. I ordered mine on-line at the address shown below. It took me at least three months to receive my Peacock, so you can see just how popular this bird is.

Related Internet site:
    NBC—http://www.nbc.com/shop/nbcstuff/index.html

Average retail price: $10

Future collectibility: As I noted previously, this is a cute and unique beanie, but it's a little expensive. Despite its price, this bean-filled character seems to be very popular. Some collectors are currently paying as much as $25 for it. Will other networks follow the beanie lead set by NBC? Will CBS come out with a "Cosby" beanie? Will ABC issue an "N.Y.P.D. Blue" set? Will Fox release a "Simpsons" set? Actually, come to think of it, the Simpsons would make a great beanie set!

NBC Beany Peacock

NBC Peacock—current value: $20

NICKELODEON RUGRATS BEANIES

The highly popular Nickelodeon cartoon "Rugrats" saw a couple of beanie sets produced in 1997. Applause made a three-beanie set called "Rugrats Bean Bags." The Applause beanies measure about 6 inches, and they are of decent quality (Applause makes several different lines of these types of beanies). Mattel, maker of the Barbie doll and Hot Wheels, issued a four-beanie set called "Holiday Rugrats Bean Bag Friends." The Mattel versions are more like what people think of as beanies—larger (about 8 inches) and plusher. The Mattel set is holiday-themed and it's top-notch quality. The costumes are great.

Tags: The hang tags include the Nickelodeon and Rugrats' logo.

Availability: The Applause versions are available at many retail outlets, but I have located the Mattel beanies only at Wal-Mart.

Average retail price: $5 for Applause; $6 for Mattel.

Internet site: Nickelodeon—http://www.nick.com/

Future collectibility: Of the two sets, the Mattel holiday beanies are of much better quality; however, the Applause beanies are cute and worth getting if you like them. "Rugrats" is one of the most popular children's cartoons on TV, and there are many, many different toys available on the market. If, in the future, people seriously collect "Rugrats" toys, look for these beanies to be a very popular item.

Nickelodeon Rugrats Beanie Characters

APPLAUSE "RUGRATS BEAN BAGS"

Reptar the dinosaur—current value: $5

Tommy—current value: $5

Spike the dog—current value: $5

MATTEL "HOLIDAY RUGRATS BEAN BAG FRIENDS"

Angelica—with angel wings; current value: $6

Chuckie—dressed as an elf; current value: $6

Tommy—dressed as Santa; current value: $6

Spike the dog—dressed as reindeer; current value: $6

PRECIOUS MOMENTS PALS

Precious Moments Pals are made by the limited-edition collectibles giant, Enesco. This set of six Pals is based on characters from stories in the Precious Moments Video series. Fine quality materials and designs boost this effort to extra nice. Enesco also makes a line of beanies called "Precious Moments Tender Tails." Precious Moments figurines, based on the artwork of Sam Butcher, were first introduced in 1979. These figurines quickly became one of the world's most popular lines of collectibles.

Note: There are variations of Dudley, Snowflake, Jeremy, and Simon (noted below). I priced them at $15+, since no market values were established for these variations. They are probably easily worth $15 each, but they could well be worth much more than that, depending on how scarce they are.

Note: A special Precious Moments Pal was produced exclusively for the 1997 Precious Moments 3rd Annual Licensee Show and Swap 'n Shop Event. The Pal was a fish named Gill, and reportedly only 1,750 were produced. Gill has been reported to sell for more than $100 on the secondary market.

Tags: The hang tags include each Pal's name, a poem and the video it's from. No tush tags.

Availability: I've seen them at several gift shops that carry Precious Moments collectibles.

Average retail price: $7

Related Internet sites:

Enesco—http://www.enesco.com/

Precious Moments Chapel—
   http://www.preciousmoments.com/

Precious Moments Collectible Treasures—
   http://www.preciousmom.com/

Future collectibility: Because these Pals are produced by Enesco, and have a tie-in to Precious Moments, consider them highly collectible. Additionally, if these characters retire at some point (and I assume that they will), they should escalate in value. How much they escalate will depend on demand and how many were made. For the serious beanie collector, Precious Moments Pals are in the must-have category.

Precious Moments Pals Characters

Dudley the dog—spot over left eye; from video: *Timmy's Special Delivery*; current value: $7

Dudley the dog—spots over both eyes, scarce; current value: $15+

Georgina the giraffe—from video: *Who's Who at the Zoo*; current value: $7

Gill the fish—current value: $100+

Hopper the bird—from video: *The Little Sparrow*; current value: $7

Jeremy the toucan—green tail; from video: *Who's Who at the Zoo*; current value: $7

Jeremy the toucan—orange tail, scarce; current value: $15+

Simon the lamb—blue face; from video: *Simon the Lamb*; current value: $7

Simon the lamb—white face, scarce; current value: $15+

Snowflake the bunny—white tail; from video: *Timmy's Gift*; current value: $7

Snowflake the bunny—pink tail, scarce; current value: $15+

PRECIOUS MOMENTS TENDER TAILS

In addition to Precious Moments Pals, Enesco has produced a bean-filled plush line called Precious Moments Tender Tails. Enesco is one of the largest makers of fine collectibles and limited edition items in the world. Released in November of 1997, Tender Tails are the first plush Precious Moments animals ever, and they are adorable! These cuties are soft and bendable, and even come with a tag that you fill out and send in to receive a personalized adoption certificate. There are six different pastel-colored plush animals, each measuring 7 inches to 8 inches long. Another set of six will be released in spring 1998, just in time for Easter: a duck, lamb, pink bunny, white bunny, brown bunny and blue bird.

Tags: The hang tags are adoption registration forms. Fill out with your name, address, and what you name your Tender Tail; send it to Enesco; and receive a personalized Tender Tails care guide and official Certificate of Adoption.

Availability: The Tender Tails can be found at stores carrying Precious Moments collectibles.

Average retail price: $7

Related Internet sites Enesco—http://www.enesco.com/
Precious Moments Collectible Treasures—
http://www.preciousmom.com/

Future collectibility: Like many beanies in this guide, Tender Tails is a set that will be sought by more than one group of collectors, enhancing the possibility of future collectibility. In this case, both beanie collectors and Precious Moments collectors will buy this set. And, like other beanies, the number produced will go a long way in determining if the value will rise.

Precious Moments Tender Tails Characters

Bear—brown; current value: $7

Elephant—blue; current value: $7

Horse—tan; current value: $7

Lion—cream; current value: $7

Pig—pink; current value: $7

Turtle—green and yellow;
current value: $7

PUFFKINS

While many manufacturers were attempting to copy the style of Ty Beanie Babies, Swibco merely mimicked the concept of making collectible bean-filled animals. Puffkins don't look like most beanie collectibles on the market. The result is nothing short of fabulous. The cute (almost square) Puffkins average about 4 1/4 inches high. Plus, they're armless—not harmless—armless. Well, they are harmless, too! Collectors seem to like Puffkins. An advantage they have over other beanies is the fact that they stand on their own very well, and can be displayed in almost perfect uniformity. The first 13 Puffkins arrived in stores in May of 1997. There were several neat variations from this original Puffkins bunch (noted in pricing section). At the time of this writing, the company had released 35 Puffkins, with another nine scheduled for February 1998 release. Snowball, the white tiger, was the first Puffkin to be retired. This was followed by the retirement of the three dinosaurs (Pickles, Dinky and Drake). These dinos are highly cute and a much recommended purchase. Swibco said that the dinos will be available through the first quarter of 1998. The company also said that it plans to retire more Puffkins in the future (all announcements of new releases and retirements are made at its Internet site).

Tags: The original Puffkins' hang tags were heart-shaped, with a dark purple border and red heart in the middle (with the "Puffkins" logo in the middle of the tag). On the inside of this tag was the name of the Puffkin, its birth date, and a poem. New hang tags began appearing in November of 1997. The dark purple border was replaced with a light purple border.

Availability: Look in Carlton Cards, Kirlin's, Coach House, Hallmark, Paper Factory, and other stores that carry various beanie toys.

Average retail price: $6

Related Internet site: Swibco—http://www.swibco.com/

Future collectibility: I rate Puffkins high in this category. Cute, and seemingly not overproduced, Puffkins could be sleepers. It might be wise to pick some up now.

Puffkins Characters

*retired

**discontinued style

Amber the brown monkey—released October 1997; birthday, 7-31-97; current value: $6

Aussie the koala—released May 1997; birthday, 5-17-97; current value: $6

Bandit the raccoon—released May 1997; birthday, 2-21-97; current value: $6

Benny the black bear—released May 1997; birthday, 1-25-97; current value: $6

Biff the buffalo—released October 1997; birthday, 7-1-94; current value: $6

Chomper the beaver—released May 1997; birthday, 2-5-97; current value: $6

Cinder the dalmatian—released October 1997; birthday, 6-30-97; current value: $6

Cinnamon the tan cat—released February 1998; birthday, 9-21-97; current value: $6

*Dinky the yellow dinosaur—released October 1997; birthday, 9-9-97; current value: $8

*Drake the red dinosaur—released October 1997; birthday, 8-21-97; current value: $8

Elly the elephant—released October 1997; birthday, 1-19-97; current value: $6

Fetch the brown dog—released May 1997; birthday, 4-7-97; current value: $6

Ginger the giraffe—released February 1998; birthday, 12-29-97; current value: $6

Gus the moose—released May 1997; birthday, 1-10-97; current value: $6

Henrietta the hippo—released October 1997; birthday, 7-21-97; current value: $6

Honey the brown bear—released May 1997; birthday, 3-27-97; current value: $6

Lancaster the lion—released August 1997; birthday, 2-27-97; current value: $6

**Lily the frog—released May 1997; birthday, 2-29-97 (limited number, bright green feet); current value: $25

Lily the frog—released May 1997; birthday, 2-28-97; dark green feet; current value: $6

Lizzy the lamb—released February 1998; birthday, 10-6-97; current value: $6

Lucky the rabbit—released May 1997; birthday, 4-23-97; current value: $6

Max the gorilla—released October 1997; birthday, 1-1-97; current value: $6

Meadow the cow—released October 1997; birthday, 3-13-97; current value: $6

Milo the black monkey—released October 1997; birthday, 8-4-97; current value: $6

Murphy the mouse—released August 1997; birthday, 5-1-97; current value: $6

Nutty the squirrel—released May 1997; birthday, 5-22-97; current value: $6

Odie the skunk—released February 1998; birthday, 12-9-97; current value: $6

Olley the owl—released October 1997; birthday, 7-7-97; current value: $6

Paws the cat—released May 1997; birthday, 6-1-97; current value: $6

Peeps the chick—released February 1998; birthday, 11-14-97; current value: $6

Percy the pig—released August 1997; birthday, 4-18-97; current value: $6

Peter the panda—released May 1997; birthday, 3-2-97; current value: $6

*Pickles the green dinosaur—released October 1997; birthday, 8-17-97; current value: $8

Quakster the duck—released August 1997; birthday, 5-2-97; current value: $6

Shadow the black cat—released February 1998; birthday, 9-4-97; current value: $6

**Shelly the turtle—released May 1997; birthday, 2-12-97 (bright green feet); current value: $25

Shelly the turtle—released May 1997; birthday, 2-12-97 (dark green feet); current value: $6

Slick the seal—released October 1997; birthday, 8-9-97; current value: $6

*Snowball the white tiger—released August 1997; birthday, 3-5-97 (black nose, first issue); current value: $35

*Snowball the white tiger—released August 1997; birthday, 3-5-97 (pink nose, second issue); current value: $12

*Snowball the white tiger—released August 1997; birthday, 3-5-97 (lavender nose, material variation); current value: $12

Tasha the white tiger—released October 1997; birthday, 11-7-97 (same style/color as Snowball with pink nose); current value: $6

Tibbs the tan rabbit—released February 1998; birthday, 10-21-97; current value: $6

Tipper the tiger—released August 1997; birthday, 4-15-97; current value: $6

Toby the whale—released February 1998; birthday, 10-11-97; current value: $6

Trixy the white monkey—released October 1997; birthday, 6-20-97; current value: $6

Tux the penguin—released October 1997; birthday, 6-12-97; current value: $6

Zack the zebra—released February 1998; birthday, 11-26-97; current value: $6

Sesame Street Bean Bags

As Sesame Street enters its 30th season, Applause has issued "Sesame Street Bean Bags." The set of five includes Big Bird, Cookie Monster, Elmo, Ernie, and Grover. Each bean bag is approximately 7 inches tall. My only question is . . . where's Bert?

Tags: The hang tags have the Sesame Street logo on the front.

Availability: The Sesame Street beanies can be found at toy stores, mass-market retailers and many local retailers.

Average retail price: $5

Internet site: Children's Television Workshop—
http://www.ctw.org/

Future collectibility: These are darling little beanies that bring many fond memories to me and I'm sure to other collectors that have watched Sesame Street. As with many collectibles, the best items are those that remind us of our childhood or of raising our own children. These may not become valuable in the future, but they are well-made and fun.

Sesame Street Bean Bag Characters

Big Bird—yellow bird; current value: $5

Cookie Monster—light blue monster; current value: $5

Elmo—red monster; current value: $5

Ernie—boy in striped shirt; current value: $5

Grover—dark blue monster; current value: $5

WARNER BROTHERS STUDIO STORE BEAN BAGS

One of my beanie favorites from 1997 is Warner Brothers Studio Store Bean Bags, featuring cartoon characters such as Bugs Bunny and Scooby Doo. These are some of the biggest and heaviest beanies featured in this book—just check out Pepe Le Pew. Similar in quality to (maybe a little better than) Disney beanies, these Warner characters are first-rate. They're a little more expensive at $7 each, but well worth it. Currently, the line is small, with just eight available.

Tags: These beanies have generic-looking Warner Brothers Studio Store tags. The names of the character are not on the tags.

Availability: These beanies are available at Warner Brothers Studio Stores and through secondary market sellers.

Average retail price: $7

Related Internet site: Warner Brothers Studio Store—
http://www.studiostores.warnerbros.com/

Future collectibility: Awfully nice, this set is already a very collectible one, and it has an excellent opportunity to gain in value over the next year, especially if the characters' styles are changed or retired. There are only eight in the set so far. Are others on the horizon? I'd bet there are more planned. Are these first eight "test" issues, such as the first 11 Disney beanies? Who knows? Keep your eyes open for possible new styles. That's all, folks!

Warner Brothers Studio Store Bean Bags Characters

Bugs Bunny—current value: $10

Commander K-9—current value: $10

Marvin the Martian—current value: $10

Pepe Le Pew—current value: $10

Scooby Doo—current value: $10

Scooby Doo—dressed as reindeer; current value: $10

Tazmanian Devil—current value: $10

Tweety Bird—current value: $10

WHERE'S WALDO BEAN-BAG TOYS

Where's Waldo? On a cereal box, that's where! Collectors can find a beanbag toy Waldo and his dog, Woof, through an offer on Quaker Oats Life cereal. To get this pair, collectors had to send two UPCs from boxes of Life or Cinnamon Life, plus $3.99 for postage. Waldo and Woof are cute and colorful, but they are of lower-end quality when compared to other beanies. Waldo is one of the taller and skinnier beanies around.

Tags: No hang tags, but they do have tush tags.

Availability: The offer for this set ends May 31, 1998.

Average retail price: $3

Future collectibility: It's too bad more effort wasn't put into these characters. The quality is such that it will be hard for them ever to become hot collectibles, even though they are recognizable characters.

Where's Waldo Bean-Bag Toy Characters

Waldo—10 1/2 inches high; current value: $4

Woof the dog—5 inches high; current value: $4

BEANIE PLUSH PRICE GUIDE

A&W Beanie Bear
A&W Bear $10

AVON FULL O' BEANS
Bernard the Bear $5
Dapper the Dinosaur 5
Juggler the Seal 5
Jumbo the Elephant 5
Lenny the Leopard 5
Mozzarella the Mouse 5
Rumply the Sharpei 5
Skips the Puppy 5
Stretch the Giraffe 5
Zoe the Zebra 5

BEANIE BABIES
*retired
**discontinued
***Price not determined at time of writing

*1997 Teddy $35
*Ally the alligator 20
Baldy the eagle 12
Batty the bat 15
Bernie the St. Bernard 10
*Bessie the cow 28
Blackie the bear 10
Blizzard the tiger 14
Bones the dog 10
Bongo the monkey, brown tail 25
Bongo the monkey, tan tail 12
*Bongo, "Nana" variation 1,225
***Britannia the bear . . . . n/a
*Bronty the brontosaurus 500
***Bruno the terrier . . . . n/a
*Bubbles the goldfish 55
*Bucky the beaver 20
*Bumble the bee 325
*Caw the crow 350
*Chilly the polar bear 875
Chip the cat 12
Chocolate the moose 11
*Chops the lamb 80
Claude the crab 12

Congo the gorilla $12
*Coral the fish 80
Crunch the shark 10
*Cubbie the bear 20
*Cubbie, "Brownie" variation 1,100
Cubbie, with May Commemorative Card 115
Cubbie with September Commemorative Card 90
Curly the bear 27
Daisy the cow 10
**Derby the horse, coarse mane 11
Derby the horse, diamond 11
Derby the horse, fine mane 700
*Digger the crab, red 45
*Digger the crab, orange 375
Doby the doberman 10
*Doodle the rooster 37
Dotty the dalmation 11
Ears the rabbit 10
Echo the dolphin 12
*Flash the dolphin 50
Fleece the lamb 12
*Flip the cat 32
Floppity the bunny 14
*Flutter the butterfly 525
Freckles the leopard 10
*Garcia the bear 75
Gobbles the turkey 15
*Goldie the goldfish 12
Gracie the swan 9
*Grunt the razorback 100
Happy the hippo, lavender 10
**Happy the hippo, grey 375
Hippity the bunny 15
***Hissy the snake . . . . n/a
*Hoot the owl 20
Hoppity the bunny 15
*Humphrey the camel 925
***Iggy the iguana . . . . n/a
Inch the inchworm 10
**Inch the inchworm, felt antennae 90
Inky the octopus, pink 12
**Inky the octopus, tan, with mouth 375
**Inky the octopus, tan, no mouth 425
Jolly the walrus 12
*Kiwi the toucan 90
*Lefty the donkey 110
*Legs the frog 20
*Libearty the bear, "Beanie" 120
*Lizzy the lizard, tie-dyed 475
*Lizzy the lizard, blue 13
**Lucky the ladybug, 21 small dots 375
**Lucky the ladybug, 7 felt spots 95
Lucky the ladybug, 11 spots 9

*Magic the dragon, light pink stitching on wings $20
*Magic the dragon, hot pink stitching on wings 50
*Manny the manatee 100
Maple the Canadian bear 90
**Maple, with Pride tag 350
Mel the koala bear 10
**Mystic the unicorn, fine mane 155
Mystic the unicorn, coarse mane/tan horn 15
Mystic the unicorn, coarse mane/iridescent horn 20
Nanook the husky 14
*Nip the cat, all gold 675
*Nip the cat, white face/belly 300
*Nip the cat, gold with white paws 13
Nuts the squirrel 9
**Patti the platypus, deep magenta 650
Patti the platypus, violet 13
Peace the bear 50
**Peanut the elephant, dark blue 1,900
Peanut the elephant, light blue 10
*Peking the panda 825
Pinchers the lobster 12
**Pinchers the lobster, "Punchers" tags 1,125
Pinky the flamingo 12
Pouch the kangaroo 10
***Pounce the cat . . . . n/a
***Prance the cat . . . . n/a
Princess the bear 275
***Puffer the puffin . . . . n/a
Pugsly the pug 14
**Quacker(s) the duck, no wings 1,225
Quackers the duck, with wings 8
*Radar the bat 80
***Rainbow the chameleon . . . . n/a
*Rex the tyrannosaurus 350
*Righty the elephant 110
Ringo the raccoon 10
Roary the lion 12
Rover the dog 10
Scoop the pelican 10
Scottie the terrier 10
*Seamore the seal 60
Seaweed the otter 12
*Slither the snake 775
**Sly the fox, brown belly 90
Sly the fox, white belly 11
***Smoochy the frog . . . . n/a
Snip the cat 10
Snort the bull 10
*Snowball the snowman 20
*Sparky the dalmation 55
*Speedy the turtle 22
Spike the rhinoceros 21
Spinner the spider 23
*Splash the whale 50
*Spook the ghost 150

*Spooky the ghost $25
*Spot the dog, no spot 1,250
*Spot the dog, with spot 25
***Spunky the cocker spaniel . . . . n/a
Squealer the pig 10
*Steg the stegosaurus 400
*Sting the ray 85
Stinky the skunk 11
***Stretch the ostrich . . . . n/a
**Stripes the tiger, orange/black, fuzzy belly 425
**Stripes the tiger, orange/black, more stripes 225
Stripes the tiger, tan/black 10
*Strut the rooster 18
*Tabasco the bull 150
*Tank the armadillo, 9-line, with ribbing 50
*Tank the armadillo, 7 line, no ribbing 100
*Tank the armadillo, 9-line, no ribbing 110
*Teddy the bear, brown, new face 50
*Teddy the bear, brown, old face 1,000
*Teddy the bear, cranberry, new face 750
*Teddy the bear, cranberry, old face 800
*Teddy the bear, jade, new face 450
*Teddy the bear, jade, old face 675
*Teddy the bear, magenta, new face 750
*Teddy the bear, magenta, old face 675
*Teddy the bear, teal, new face 825
*Teddy the bear, teal, old face 750
*Teddy the bear, violet, new face 900
*Teddy the bear, violet, old face 675
*Trap the mouse 550
Tuffy the terrier 12
*Tusk the walrus 65
*Tusk with "Tuck" swing tag 80
Twigs the giraffe 12
Valentino the Bear 22
*Velvet the panther 23
Waddle the penguin 10
Waves the whale 12
*Web the spider 625
Weenie the dachshund 15
Wrinkles the bulldog 10
Ziggy the zebra, thin stripes 10
Ziggy the zebra, thick stripes 10
**Zip the cat, all black 1,250
**Zip the cat, white face/belly 325
Zip the cat, black with white paws 13

BEANIE BABIES: TEENIE BEANIE BABIES
Complete set of 10 (all are retired) $75
Chocolate 8

Chops	$10
Goldie	8
Lizz	7
Patti	10
Pinky	14
Quacks	7
Seamore	8
Snort	7
Speedy	8

BEANPALS

"HOTSY SPOTSY" BEANPALS

Cheddar the mouse	$5
Crumpet the frog	5
Holy Cow the cow	5
Hot Diggity the dog	5
Hot Dog the dog	5
Hot Frog the frog	5
Hot Spot the dog	5
Hotsy the bunny	5
Pigsby the pig	5
Pigsy the pig	5
Sharper the dog	5
Sharpy the dog	5
Silly Cow the cow	5
Spotso the hippo	5

"ORIGINAL" BEANPALS

Alley the cat	5
Andy Pandy the panda bear	5
Bass the dog	5
Beau the panther	5
Beavis the bear	5
Bernie the dog	5
Birdy the bird	5
Blueberry the frog	5
Boomer the kangaroo	5
Bronto the dinosaur	5
Bronty the dinosaur	5
Bubba the fish	5
Bubble the fish	5
Bubble Gum the bear	5
Bud the bear	5
Buddy the frog	5
Bumble the bee	5
Butch the dog	5
Butterball the bear	5

"LIMITED EDITION" BEANPAL

142

BEAN SPROUTS

retired

Acorn the squirrel	$4
Alex the alligator	4
Ariel the ostrich	4
*Bandit the raccoon	5
*Berry the neon bear	6
Billy the blue jay	4
*Bobo the black bear	6
Boris the spider—see Widow	
Bossie the cow	4
Bruno the tie-dyed brontosaurus	4
Bubba the tie-dyed T. rex	4
Bubble Gum the neon pig	4
Bucky the beaver	4
Buford the brown pup	4
Buttercup the neon cow	4
Button the snowman	4
Casanova the Valentine bear	4
*Claw the crab	5
Cleo the neon cat	4
Cloppy the horse	4
Cottontail the bunny, pink	4
Cottontail the bunny, white	4
Daisy the tie-dyed cow—see Sunshine	
Danny the dalmatian	4
Dash the dolphin	4
Domino the Orca whale	4
*Dotty the ladybug	7
Dundee the koala bear	4
Felix the neon frog	4
Finster the tropical fish	4
Freida the goldfish	4
*Gentle the lamb	5
Godfrey the ghost	4
Grace the angel	4
Grand Slam the baseball	4
Gus the gorilla	4
Honey the bumblebee	4
Hornsby the rhino	4
Howie the wolf	4
J.R. the terrier	4
Jumbo the elephant	4
Kick the soccer ball	4
Kris Santa	4
Lana the lobster	4
Lenny the leopard	4
Leo the lion	4
Lilly the tie-dyed frog	4

Widow the spider, Boris hang tag	$4
Wing the Pegasus	4
Winston the bulldog	4
Yakky the parrot	4
Zak the zebra	4
Zelda the witch	4

CHEF JR. BEANBAG BUDDIES

Christy the sea horse	$4
Jumbo the whale	4
Rex the tyrannosaurus rex	4
Rigatoni the dog	4
Sharkeel the shark	4
Steggy the stegosaurus	4

CLIFFORD THE BIG RED DOG

Clifford the Big Red Dog	$10

COCA-COLA BEAN BAG PLUSH

retired

*1ST SERIES, "SPRING 1997"

Penguin with delivery hat	$8
Polar Bear with Coca-Cola baseball hat	8
Polar Bear	8
Polar Bear with Coca-Cola shirt	8
Polar Bear with red bow	8
Seal with baseball hat	8

*2ND SERIES, "HOLIDAY"

Penguin with Coca-Cola stocking hat	8
Polar Bear with Coca-Cola stocking hat	8
Polar Bear with plaid bow tie	8
Polar Bear with red bow	8
Seal with red and white scarf	8
Seal with red and white stocking hat	8

3RD SERIES, "HERITAGE"

Coca-Cola can with hat	7
Polar Bear with hat and shirt	7
Polar Bear with hat and bow tie	7
Moose	7
Seal with hat	7
Walrus	7

DISNEY MINI BEAN BAGS

*retired

"101 DALMATIANS"
101 Dalmatians pup—Style 1 . . . . $40
101 Dalmatians pup—Style 2 25
101 Dalmatians pup—Style 3 10
*Jewel 15
Lucky 10

"ALADDIN"
Abu 10
Genie 10

"ARISTOCATS"
Marie 10

"BAMBI"
Bambi 10
Flower 10
Thumper 10

"FLUBBER"
*Flubber 12

"HERCULES"
**Pain . . . . 12+
**Panic . . . . 12+
*Pegasus 15
**available by pre-ordering "Hercules" video before Feb. 2, 1998

"LADY AND THE TRAMP"
Lady 10
Tramp 10

"LION KING"
Nala 10
Pumbaa 10
Simba 10
Timon 10

"LITTLE MERMAID FRIENDS"
*Flounder—Style 1 18
*Flounder—Style 2 12
*Sebastian—Style 1 20
*Sebastian—Style 2 12

"MICKEY & FRIENDS"
Daisy 10
Donald 10
Goofy—Style 1 25
Goofy—Style 2 10
Mickey—Style 1 45

"Toy Story"

Alien $10
Buzz Lightyear 10
Woody 10

Energizer Bunny Bean Bag Toy

Energizer Bunny $10

General Mills Big G Breakfast Babies

Chip the Cookie Hound $6
Count Chocula 6
Honey Nut Cheerios Bee 6
Lucky the Leprechaun 6
Sonny the Cuckoo Bird 6
Trix Rabbit 6
Wendell the Baker 6

Grateful Dead Beanie Bears

Althea $12
Bertha 12
Cassidy 12
Cosmic Charlie 12
Delilah 12
Jack Straw 12
St. Stephen 12
Samson 12
Stagger Lee 12
Sugaree 12
Tennessee Jed 12

Gund

"Animal Beanies"

Dahling the ostrich $7
Flash the frog (all green) 7
Flash the frog (green with yellow belly) 7
Flash the frog (green with light green belly) 7
Mooky the walrus 7
Puddles the dog 7
Rainbow Racer the turtle 7
Slider the floppy bear 7
Snuffy the sitting bear (chocolate brown) 7

Snuffy the sitting bear (tan brown) $7
Tender Teddy the bear 7
Tinkle the inch worm 7

"BABAR"
Babar the elephant 12
Celeste the elephant 12

"BABE"
Babe the pig 8
Ferdinand the goose 8
Fly the dog 8
Maa the sheep 8

"BARNEY"
Baby Bop the green dinosaur 8
Barney the purple dinosaur 8

"CLASSIC POOH"
Pooh the bear 12
Eeyore the donkey 12
Kanga the kangaroo 12
Tigger the tiger 12
Piglet the Pig (grayish-green body) 12
Piglet the Pig (soft green body) 12

"CURIOUS GEORGE"
Curious George the monkey 12

"DILBERT"
Boss 10
Catbert the cat 10
Dilbert 10
Dogbert the dog 10
Ratbert the rat 10

HALLMARK'S BABY NIKKI
Baby Nikki $5

HARLEY-DAVIDSON BEAN BAG PLUSH
Big Twin bear $8
Motorhead bear 8
Punky pig 8
Racer pig 8
Rachet pig 8
Roamer bear 8

KELLOGG'S BEAN BAG BREAKFAST BUNCH

Cornelius $7
Crackle! 7
Dig 'Em 7
Pop! 7
Snap! 7
Tony the Tiger 7
Toucan Sam 7

MCDONALD'S FLOPPY DOLLS

Grimace $5
Hamburglar 5
Ronald McDonald 5

MEANIES

Armydillo Dan $6
Bart the Elephart 6
Boris the Mucousaurus 6
Fi & Do the Dalmutation 6
Hurley the Pukin' Toucan 6
Matt the Fat Bat 6
Mystery Meanie . . . . 10+
Navy Seal 6
Otis the Octapunk 6
Peter the Gotta Peegull 6
Sledge the Hammered Head Shark 6
Snake Eyes Jake 6
Splat the Road Kill Kat 6

NBC BEANY PEACOCK

NBC Peacock $20

NICKELODEON RUGRATS BEANIE CHARACTERS

APPLAUSE "RUGRATS BEAN BAGS"

Reptar the dinosaur $5
Tommy 5
Spike the dog 5

MATTEL "HOLIDAY RUGRATS BEAN BAG FRIENDS"

Angelica $6
Chuckie 6
Tommy 6
Spike the dog 6

PRECIOUS MOMENTS PALS

Dudley the dog, spot over left eye $7
Dudley the dog, spots over both eyes . . . . 15+
Georgina the giraffe 7
Gill the fish . . . . 100+
Hopper the bird 7
Jeremy the toucan, green tail 7
Jeremy the toucan, orange tail . . . . 15+
Simon the lamb, blue face 7
Simon the lamb, white face . . . . 15+
Snowflake the bunny, white tail 7
Snowflake the bunny, pink tail . . . . 15+

PRECIOUS MOMENTS TENDER TAILS

Bear $7
Elephant 7
Horse 7
Lion 7
Pig 7
Turtle 7

PUFFKINS

*retired
**discontinued

Amber the brown monkey $6
Aussie the koala 6
Bandit the raccoon 6
Benny the black bear 6
Biff the buffalo 6
Chomper the beaver 6
Cinder the dalmatian 6
Cinnamon the tan cat 6
*Dinky the yellow dinosaur 8
*Drake the red dinosaur 8
Elly the elephant 6

Fetch the brown dog $6

Ginger the giraffe 6

Gus the moose 6

Henrietta the hippo 6

Honey the brown bear 6

Lancaster the lion 6

**Lily the frog, 2-29-97, bright green feet 25

Lily the frog, 2-28-97, dark green feet 6

Lizzy the lamb 6

Lucky the rabbit 6

Max the gorilla 6

Meadow the cow 6

Milo the black monkey 6

Murphy the mouse 6

Nutty the squirrel 6

Odie the skunk 6

Olley the owl 6

Paws the cat 6

Peeps the chick 6

Percy the pig 6

Peter the panda 6

*Pickles the green dinosaur 8

Quakster the duck 6

Shadow the black cat 6

**Shelly the turtle, bright green feet 25

Shelly the turtle, dark green feet 6

Slick the seal 6

*Snowball the white tiger, black nose 35

*Snowball the white tiger, pink nose 12

*Snowball the white tiger, lavender nose 12

Tasha the white tiger 6

Tibbs the tan rabbit 6

Tipper the tiger 6

Toby the whale 6

Trixy the white monkey 6

Tux the penguin 6

Zack the zebra 6

SESAME STREET BEAN BAGS

Big Bird $5

Cookie Monster 5

Elmo 5

Ernie 5

Grover 5

WARNER BROTHERS STUDIO STORE BEAN BAGS

Bugs Bunny $10
Commander K-9 10
Marvin the Martian 10
Pepe Le Pew 10
Scooby Doo 10
Scooby Doo (reindeer) 10
Tazmanian Devil 10
Tweety Bird 10

WHERE'S WALDO BEAN-BAG TOY

Waldo $4
Woof the dog 4

BEANIE INDEX

ABOUT THE AUTHOR

A long-time antiques and collectibles enthusiast, Shawn Brecka has written a book entitled *Collecting in Cyberspace* and articles that have appeared in the *Antique Trader Weekly* and Warman's *Today's Collector* magazines. In addition, she developed electronic communication networks and support materials for professional organizations, including the American Society for Quality Control. When she's not surfing the net or searching for beanie plush, Shawn is busy adding to her other collections of ruby red glass, vintage purses, beaded collars, and sewing items.

we write the books on collectibles

all kinds of collectibles

dolls, pottery, Star Wars, Beatles memorabilia, glass, comics, Coca-Cola collectibles, marionettes, autographs, baseball, animal stars, golf balls, die-cast vehicles. . .